Derek Cajun

Gentleman's Guide to Online Dating

Gentleman's Guide to Online Dating by Derek Cajun

Love Systems Publishing, Christoph Lymbersky, Luetkensallee 41, 22041 Hamburg. Classic Books Publishing is a label of the MLP Management Laboratory Press UG, registered in Hamburg, Germany.

Publication date: April 2012, Hamburg, Germany

Registered with:
ISBN-Agentur für die Bundesrepublik Deutschland in der MVB
Marketing- und Verlagsservice des Buchhandels GmbH
Bibliografische Information der Deutschen Nationalbibliothek:
Die Deutsche Nationalbibliothek verzeichnet diese Publikation in der Deutschen Nationalbibliografie; detaillierte bibliografische Daten sind im Internet über http://dnb.d-nb.de abrufbar.

Front Cover Picture: © MLP Management Laboratory Press
                                & Love Systems Inc., © Maksim Samasiuk,
                                © jameschipper
Interior Pictures: : © Love Systems Inc.
Text Layout: : © MLP Management Laboratory Press

When ordering this title, use ISBN: 978-3-94157931-6

Derek Cajun

Table of Contents

About the Author

Cajun is an instructor for Love Systems, a company devoted to helping men improve their love life by helping them understand women and dating. For more than five years Cajun has taught seminars all over the world specializing in concepts such as body language, inner confidence, identity, flirting and overcoming fear. Cajun, along with Love Systems, has been featured on television programs such as Dr. Phil, ABC Nightline, The Tyra Banks Show, Cityline, Sex Matters, and Keys to the VIP and is widely recognized as one of the best in his field. In 2010 he released a home study course on DVD entitled *Beyond Words* which has since sold thousands of copies and garnered rave reviews for being one of the premiere products for learning attractive body language. This is Cajun's first book and is a culmination of over four years' worth of experimentation successfully using online dating sites.

Foreword

I heard a funny one-liner years ago that went something like: "Online dating; it may as well be legal prostitution!" The funny part is that my immediate reaction to hearing that was "Shit. I gottta look into this online dating stuff!" Being a twenty-two year old out of work actor frustrated with women can make you think like that.

The story of how I gotten good at online game is actually a little amusing. You see, several years ago, before I became an instructor for Love Systems, I had gotten to a point in my game where getting a woman's number was fairly easy. I'd often come home with the numbers of several women who I had met that night and those numbers would eventually turn into dates. This amounted to me going on a lot of dates and the problem I kept having was that I didn't really know what to do on the date. Sure, I could talk a woman's head off in the bar, charm her and her friends and be the centre of attention, but on the date I would fizzle. I figured the whole problem was due to a lack of experience, so in order to learn how to master dates I decided that I would try to go on as many dates as possible until I had the whole process down. This is why I turned to online dating.

The allure of online dating for me was that I could do most of my grunt work, that is, setting up dates, from home. I didn't really care about the quality of the women; as long as they weren't embarrassingly unattractive, I would give everyone a fair chance. Besides, all I was really trying to learn was how to be an awesome *first* date. Beyond that I wasn't really interested in anything. I knew that using an online dating site meant that I could go out at night to practice in the bars, and then come home and work on online dating for an hour or two and then go to bed. The payoff seemed like it would be time well spent if it meant more dates. After spending a few weeks trying out different types of messages, I had figured out what to message women in order to get their attention, and eventually their phone numbers, but this was just the beginning. The real value of online dating came later when I realized how to construct my profile so that I could get women to message me!

So after those first few weeks of learning I started to go on dates about three to four times a week with women I was meeting off dating sites. This continued for about two to three months and there were a couple weeks in there when I had a date scheduled every single night. To say that I took a good crack at online dating would be an understatement. I *lived and breathed* online dating for a good few months, and in the process got ridiculously good at it. Not only that, but I've been continuing to practice and tinker with my system since I started, so this book literally encompasses *years* worth of insights related to online dating.

So let's talk a little about the value of online dating and what the information in this book should mean to you in the end. First, online dating should not be used as an excuse to stay in. The whole point of your online dating profile should be: YOU DON'T NEED TO USE AN ONLINE DATING SITE TO MEET WOMEN. The easiest way to accomplish that goal is to actually go out and meet women. You will also find that if you're not out on a consistent basis practising your social skills, you will almost assuredly mess the date up in the end anyways, so please, don't turn into lame internet dating site guy... women can spot them from a mile away.

The real purpose of this book, and online dating itself, is to help *enrich* your life with women, not compensate for a lack thereof. When I first started playing around with dating sites I made myself a promise that I would only ever use the dating site as a way to augment my existing abilities, and as a way to stay sharp when I couldn't go out. It was a great deal for me: I spend an hour or two crafting a perfect profile, upload some nice pics, check my inbox once or twice a day to keep me at the top of the available list (more on that later), and then have one or two women a day message me based on my profile. Now, most of those women won't be anything special, but over the long run this ended up getting me about two to three women a week who were very attractive and who were essentially served to me on a silver platter. That's a pretty good deal when you consider how little work is involved to attain that.

I've been working on this book for several years, and even if I managed to convince you that after reading through this and taking my advice that you could have tons of gorgeous women messaging you, that still wouldn't be reason enough for me to recommend it. I needed to sweeten the deal. I wanted my first book to be so good that it would be worth its weight in gold. So this book not only explains *in detail* how to write your "about me," which pictures to use and why, and everything else that goes along with creating a killer dating profile, but I've also included every other tool, tip and tactic you will need to go from logging into the dating site to having a beautiful woman in your bed in the shortest time possible.

As an added bonus I've included special guest chapters by two of my good friends and fellow Love Systems instructors. A chapter on "Phone Game" has been included by Tenmagnet, who has been touring the world the past few years giving sold-out talks about how important the first phone call is and how to properly set up the first date. And a chapter titled "Intro to Online Dating" by Keychain, which goes over his own insights into online dating which he has been toying with since I introduced it to him a few years ago. I've also included my famous version of the "Question Game Routine," which has been unavailable for anyone other than seminar attendees up until this point and has been one of the highest rated presentations the past few years at the annual Love Systems Super Conference: (a conference held in Las Vegas every October featuring presentations and workshops from all the Love Systems instructors). This routine has been a closely guarded secret of mine for the past few years and with good reason; it's the most powerful routine I know, and is the only thing I teach that I can reliably (and consistently) guarantee will create an exciting, arousing conversation that will lead to an unforgettable first date.

So there you have it, I hope you enjoy my book and I hope that it helps bring you the success with women that you deserve.

Online Dating Stigma

(And Some Warnings)

Whether you agree with it or not, online dating still has a bit of a stigma attached to it. Many women would not feel comfortable telling their friends that the guy they're dating was someone they had met off of an internet dating site. In fact, I've had several women tell me precisely those words after I'd been on a date or two with them. The reason why is pretty obvious: most people don't want to feel as if they need to resort to the internet to find a date. The good news is that, as a guy, we can use this to our advantage (more on that later). The bad news is that as far along as internet dating has come, it still carries those old stereotypes, and wears them rather proudly in some cases...

I'm not going to lie; you're almost definitely going to meet some unstable women if you play the internet dating game long enough. It's gotten much better over the years, but the ratio is still a great deal higher than what you'd find in your average bar on a Saturday night. The good thing is that most of these women are avoidable if you pay attention to the key factors and warning signs. I'll list some below:

   Always ask yourself the question: "Why?" What has motivated this person to use an internet dating site? Is she incredibly beautiful? If she appears to be someone who would have a lot of options in reality, why then is she resorting to online dating? Read her profile; what's the reason she lists for trying out the dating site? Friends recommended it? Just trying it out? These clues can save you a lot of headaches later on, so pay attention and try to get an understanding of her motivations.

Are her pictures hiding something? If all she has are head shots then there's a good chance that she may have some weight issues. I had one woman who never showed anything below her waist. I later found out that she was missing a leg, which isn't the most terrible thing, I mean Paul McCartney was with a woman with one leg for years and he could have had any woman, but it just goes to show you that if women can omit something physical in their pictures, they probably will.

Is she emphasizing her sexuality a little too much? If all of her shots are showing off her cleavage and ass, then you're most likely going to meet someone who has had to resort to using her body to get ahead her whole life. These women can be fun for a little while, but it grows old pretty quickly.

Is she alone in all her pictures? You might be dealing with a recluse, or maybe someone who is lacking in social intelligence. Beautiful women come in all flavours; don't be tricked into thinking that just because she's attractive she's a normal social person.

Even if they pass all these warning signs they may still have undesirable qualities that are elusive. I'll talk about digital bouncing later on in the book, which is a good way to screen potentials more thoroughly. This may sound a bit paranoid, but the truth is that I'm speaking from hindsight; I've had two stalkers from meeting women online and they're not fun. Looking back, if I had known all the warning signs I would have been able to avoid it. So believe me, it's best to be over cautious.

You may also find that certain cities are better for online dating than others. When I lived in Toronto, a city known for being quite social and having a great nightlife, the ratio of unstable to normal women was pretty high. Now that I live in Vancouver, a city known for its crippling social anxiety and near non-existent nightlife, I've found many more normal women online and far less unstable ones. Women tend to turn to dating sites for a myriad of reasons but it's usually due to a lack of options. So if your city is known for being friendly and easy to meet people in, you may find the online dating pool a little stagnant.

Dating Sites

Which ones to use and why?

I've purposely divided this book into two parts for the use of dating sites. The first part deals with sites that are used explicitly for meeting women who are looking to meet men such as PlentyofFish.com and OKCupid.com and the second part deals with social networking sites such as Facebook and Myspace which are mainly used for transitioning women from the dating site. Which dating site to use then is our first order of business; it's also tremendously important as it will dictate the pool of women from which we can draw.

When you get down to it all of the dating sites can fit into one of two categories: free sites and pay sites. Although the pay sites tend to advertise about having more quality women and women who are taking internet dating a little more seriously, I've found that most of the pay sites fluff their listed profiles with fake women (which are quite easy to spot as they contain generic profiles with no personal information and often have professional pictures) and contain a lot of women who are either older (which may or may not be a bad thing for you) or are desperate. They also list expired profiles of women who may have not logged in for years. Oh yeah and you have to pay too. Having said that, there are some that friends of mine have recommended and that I've heard good things about but they seem to be few and far between and I've found that the free sites are often better anyway, so it's really no contest. The deciding factor for which site you turn to should really have more to do with where you live, and which sites have active listings in your area.

There are some sites that are targeted for specific sub-groups of men. For instance J-date is a site that caters specifically to Jewish males and only features listed profiles of Jewish women. So if your nagging Jewish mother is always pestering you to find a nice Jewish woman, then this may be a site you would like to consider. There are others as well though; for instance I've seen a couple sites that cater specifically to men who have large incomes. Although I've never signed up to check these sites out (I'm not rich) they seem to be a bit of a trap from what I can tell. Sure you get to have women know that you're loaded before the date, but does that really give you an advantage on a site where everyone is presumably rich? I imagine if you're older there would be a certain appeal to the site, since security through monetary means could be a relevant, although somewhat disheartening quality that older women may be looking for, but I'm guessing you would be knee-deep in gold diggers before you found any respectable women on the site, so proceed with caution.

The best sites I've found so far, and the ones that I still use to this day are PlentyofFish.com and OKCupid.com. They haven't endorsed me or anything, they just really are the best sites for meeting women that I've found. They're free, have plenty of listings in just about every city that I've used them in (which are many worldwide) and have a number of features that I find very useful and advantageous to people who know how to use them.

Chapter 1 Profile

I think the biggest mistake that most guys tend to make when deciding to try out online dating is that they take the whole thing seriously. I've seen too many guys who design their online profiles as if they're job applications. Not a good idea. Remember earlier when I talked about asking the question "Why?" with regards to what women's profiles communicate about what their reason to try online dating is? Well keep in mind that women are doing the exact same thing for your profile. If they get the impression that you're turning to online dating because you can't meet women in your everyday life, then they're going to assume you're a loser, even if your profile lists lots of great things about you. Understand that even if women have trouble meeting guys in their everyday life and feel that using online dating will help them, they don't want others to suspect that they need it. Often they sign up and convince themselves that they're not creating a profile out of desperation, but out of curiosity or a recommendation from friends and if they read your profile and it reminds them of this desperation, they will next you.

As part of the research for this book I've watched many of my female friends peruse male profiles on internet dating sites, and the results were interesting. If the profile was funny, and quirky, often they would be more inclined to message him. However, if the profile was written too seriously, or devoid of humour they would become bored and next him. Even if he was a good looking guy with a nicely written profile, the mere fact that he was taking the whole thing seriously turned them off. Now, this may not be the case with women who have come to terms with their need to use online dating sites, but the most attractive women are rarely that type.

Most dating sites follow the same guidelines for the construction of your profile. They all include pictures, a bio or "about me," and most include a separate section for physical facts (age, height, race) as well as interests or hobbies. I'm going to get into all of these individually in this section and hopefully give you a good idea of what your profile should look and read like.

Pictures

Nearly every dating site is going to have a section in your profile for pictures. Some will allow more than others, and some sites have a private section for pictures that can only be seen with your permission. The one thing their picture sections all have in common though, is that they all have a main picture. This is the first photo women see when they look at your profile and it's also the picture that is going to show up when women look at a page full of tiny photos representing men in their area. Your main picture is going to be your thumbnail and it's going to be the one and only picture which will entice women to check out your profile; because of that it is the most important picture in your entire set. Since this is literally the first thing women will notice on your profile, let's tackle it first.

Profile Picture

Now since, as I said, your profile picture is the most important, there are a couple things that you're going to want to do differently with it compared to the rest of your pictures. The first thing is that, since it's primarily going to be viewed as a thumbnail, your best bet is to have a fairly close-up picture of your face. That way they get a pretty good view of your mug before they even visit your profile. But, you're probably wondering "What if I'm ugly as fuck!?" That's OK, I'm going to go over a few ways you can make your ugly mug look a hell of a lot more attractive.

The easiest way to make yourself look more attractive is to have a professional photographer take the photo. Now, I'm not saying you should go out and hire somebody, although some of you may have to resort to that if you have no other options, but most people should have at least one friend who shelled out the extra couple hundred when purchasing a digital camera and got the upgraded pro cam with the detachable lens. Make friends with that guy. The new digital cameras these days can take amazing pictures and are a hell of a lot better than your 4.0 megapixel Sony from 6 years ago. If you've got the cash yourself and have some friends or family with an interest in photography, the new Canon SLRs are amazing, but even the cheaper Canon Powershots take very impressive pictures and offer a lot of bang for your buck. I recommend getting a new one though as the picture technology has increased tremendously in the past few years.

If you're instructing your photographer tell him that you'd like to use a shallow focus on your face, if possible. All this means is that there will be a very small depth of field in the picture. Your face will be pronounced against the background and stand out more, as well as having a flattening effect that many cinematographers use on celebrities to hide imperfections in the face. There are actually some actors who refuse to be photographed unless it's in a small depth of field, as it can hide things like big noses, overbites and other facial imperfections. The easiest way to attain this effect if you're doing it yourself is to stand as far away as you can from the camera and have the zoom maximized for a close up (avoid digital zooms though) and focus in on your face. The background should appear blurry, with your face in focus.

On your end, make sure that your hair looks good, you're wearing the clothes that best communicate who you are, and that you're smiling. There are some other tricks you can use though. Firstly, don't look at the camera. That may sound weird, but they actually did a study with dating sites that found that women tend to click on men who are not looking at the camera quite a bit more than those who are. I suppose the obvious reason would be because it communicates non-neediness but the psychology of it isn't that important; just try to focus on something other than the camera. Don't stare blindly into the distance, but focus on something else, as if deep in thought. Make sure your face is facing the lens though. If you'd like a breakdown of what you're communicating by the look, here's what I've found with my studies into it:

Eyes looking above the camera = Dreamer, religious, happy, content.

Eyes looking down = Deep, emotional, artist, interesting.

Eyes looking to the sides = Sense of humour, trickster, cocky.

Choose the one that best suits you if you're clueless as to what to do with your eyes. Remember to smile and try not to tilt your head too much; only your eyes should be moved.

Taking advantage of forty-five degree angles can help as well. It's a well known fact that when you're positioning your body at a forty-five degree angle you actually are perceived as more attractive. The Greeks would carve their marble statues of male heroes and gods positioned in forty-five degree angles to emphasize their courage, presence and virility. Filmmakers and photographers employ this tactic all the time to make their stars stand out amongst others in the frame. The angle communicates that you are someone who is meant to be admired and gazed upon. Position your shoulders at a forty-five degree angle to the camera and relax your body. This promotes an aura of confidence, masculinity, and virility.

The last piece of advice I'll give you for your profile picture is to make it stand out. There are a number of ways to do this. Employing some type of filter is an easy way to make a picture stand out from a sea of others; I'd recommend black & white over more in-your-face type filters. I've had success with film-grain, letterbox, and high contrast filters. Just don't go too crazy with the stained glass, etch-a-sketch, lens flare, etc. effects. I'd definitely recommend picking up Photoshop (not just for the filters either); you can employ all sorts of tools to enhance your pictures through colour correction, cropping, and touch-ups. Nothing is worse than an overly Photoshopped picture and it's a lot more evident than you might think.

Lighting is also something you're going to want to take advantage of since it can make or break a picture. There are plenty of lighting tutorials on the internet that I would recommend checking out if you'd really like to pimp out your photos, but I'll give you a few tips to get you started. Going through your pictures you've probably noticed that you look better in some than in others; this is usually because of the lighting. Some people have features that are more flattering when properly lit. For instance, if you have deep set eyes, and you're lit predominantly from overhead lighting, it can give you a sickly appearance. A flash will fix this, but it can also create other problems like making you look pale (if you're lighter skinned), or it could reflect and make your skin look greasy, especially if the shot was taken too close. So if using a flash, find the proper distance where it's not too dark but also not too blown out.

The easiest way to get good light in a photo is natural light. Go outdoors, but not in direct sun. Find a shady spot, either in a doorway or behind a building. There will still be shadow, but it will be more subtle. Most people look best in indirect or soft light coming straight at them. In this cast the light source, even though indirect, would be directly behind the photographer. You can try back light and side lighting also. Right around sunset and sunrise provide the best lighting, because the light is coming from that entire side of the sky, so your face gets lit up nice and evenly and the shadows are soft. You can also take the picture indoors near a large window, but again not in direct light. Also if there's a lot of light and you are getting a lot of shadow, you want the light to be either behind you or facing you, not to the side. Try both.

If you are going to take a shot indoors, it's good to get light from multiple angles. Move a few lamps around and experiment. You can try with and without the flash as well. How the picture turns out is going to depend on what types of lights you have and what kind of camera, so you really need to experiment and try different things.

Another way to make it stand out is the context of the picture itself. In one of my most successful profile pictures I'm wearing an eye patch, leaned back on a couch with a seductive nonchalant facial expression drinking a beer. The context is quite unflattering in that I look like a slob; my belly is showing and I'm not even trying to appear attractive, but that's actually the most attractive aspect of the picture. I've had numerous women comment on that photo saying that I looked so smug in my dishevelled state, that that's what made them want to click on me; I looked like a character! Finding photos with that sort of quality may take some trial and error so be sure to experiment with your photos. Most dating sites have a feature that lets you see how many women have viewed your profile, so try out different profile pictures and find out which one gives you the most views. You could also use a site such as hotornot.com and submit your pictures to see which one gets the best rating. Sometimes the most unexpected pictures can give you the best reactions, simply because they communicate something that you weren't aware of. Experiment experiment experiment!

The Other Pictures

OK, so we've got the profile picture taken care of, great! Now it's time to work on the rest of the pictures. Try to have enough pictures on your profile so that the women can get a good view of who you are and what your life is like. In fact, the sole purpose of the rest of your photos is to paint a picture of who you are in the most positive light. I'd recommend having at least six to eight pictures; this is really to your advantage, since every picture is an opportunity to seduce. If you only have a few pictures that meet the criteria I'm going to explain, that's fine, just add more as you get them. I'm going to get into a number of different tactics you can employ to make sure that the picture you paint is a good one, so let's tackle them one at a time.

One of the first things you're going to want to communicate with your pictures is that you have a social life outside of the internet. This hits on the "I don't need to resort to internet dating to meet women" mentality I mentioned earlier, but it also goes a bit deeper than that. Women are social creatures by nature and find men who have a large social group, or "social proof" as we call it, more attractive. Try not to have any pictures, outside of your profile picture, feature you alone unless it's communicating something positive (which I'll get into later). What I mean by that is, if the only thing your picture communicates is that you were alone in the picture, not travelling, not doing something exciting, not witnessing an interesting event, then it's not an ideal picture. This may mean that you need to start taking more pictures when you're with your friends. That's a good habit to get into. I started bringing a camera around whenever I was out with friends and after a few weeks had acquired quite a few pictures to work with. As I mentioned before, if you're serious about online dating then getting a nice camera is a worthy investment.

Now, simply having pictures of yourself with a bunch of friends around, although fine, isn't necessarily the best way to communicate your social value. There are a couple ways you're going to want to maximize this "social proof" aspect of your personality. The first is to have your picture define your role within your social group. Simply being in a group of people doesn't really communicate much other than "I have friends." Try to find a picture where you are the centre of attention. Maybe telling a joke and having everyone laughing, or doing something interesting with friends cheering you on. Try to put yourself in these situations and hand off your camera to a friend to capture the moment. You don't necessarily have to wait for these moments to happen though, you can stage them if you're creative. Sometimes I would hand off my camera to a waitress or passer-by and ask them to take a picture of me and my friends. When we posed I would say something like "hey guys, let's not pose with fake smiles, let's just pretend were all having a hilariously awesome time. Fake smiles look so lame!" Then as everyone was smiling and looking as if they're having fun, I would mime as if I was talking; the result would be a picture that appeared as if I was entertaining a group of friends.

It's also a good idea to make sure your social group in the pictures isn't predominantly a man-party. Nothing says desperate more than a massive group of guys looking to pick up chicks. Try to invite some female friends out and incorporate them into the pictures so that it doesn't appear as if you have no female friends. This communicates several things. Firstly it makes you seem like someone who probably isn't creepy (which is a huge concern for women meeting guys online) and secondly it makes it appear as if you have options. Women are going to naturally assume you're hooking up with the women in your pictures, even if the context is friendly. So women in the pictures will make you appear more content with your current situation and less likely to need online dating. If you don't have too many female friends, or none that you would want to be seen in pictures with, you may want to consider alternative routes. "Hiring" women to escort you to venues may be a financially viable option for you, just remember to be honest and forthcoming with your intentions so no laws are broken, ahem.   Speaking of women in your photos...

Most guys realize that having pictures of them with women is quite important since it hints that they may have options; that much is obvious from all the male profiles I've seen. How you go about trying to communicate this with your photos is where I see a lot of men run into problems. Most women will find a picture of you groping, or making out with a woman pretty lame, even if the women in the pictures are hot. The idea here is that it should appear as if the women are hitting on YOU, not the other way around. There's a certain amount of classiness you should follow when it comes to choosing these photos as well, since women are going to know that you specifically chose the photos that you did. A photo showing you being groped by a woman while you look disinterested may communicate that you are preselected, but it also communicates that you feel the need to explicitly communicate that. Much better would be a photo where a woman is casually flirting with you, maybe a hand on your shoulder while laughing, or her body close and facing yours while you appear more neutrally positioned, or centred.

The identity that you want to communicate in relation to the women in your life is this: You have many women in your life that love, admire and flirt with you. This makes you appear as the object of desire in your social group. One of my favourite pictures that I still use in my profile to this day features me in a room with two attractive women: one is laughing and the other is looking at me pointing to her lips as if to say "Please kiss me!" The look on my face says "Sweetheart, I know you love me, but restrain yourself." That's a very powerful frame that's established in just one picture. As I mentioned before, you don't have to wait for these situations to arise, you can simply stage them. Just tell your female friends that you need some photos for your online dating profile (or just say it's for a project if you'd rather not admit to online dating) and tell them how you'd like the shots set up.

Alright, so we've established that you have friends, you're the centre of your social group, and that women love you. What else? Well, we're going to need to establish an identity with your photos. Your identity is essentially like the cover of a book in that women are going to judge you based on it, so you want it to portray you in the best possible light. Your interests and hobbies are a good place to start: what do you do for fun? Sports? Music? Art? Throw up a picture of you partaking in those activities. Maybe playing a show with your friends, competing in some sort of tournament, or finishing the last brush stroke on your masterpiece. You want to communicate your exciting hobbies as well, so don't put up pictures of you playing video games, reading comic books or masturbating. Those don't count. If you don't have anything that is interesting then maybe you should take something up! Take music lessons, improvisation classes, or martial arts training and get some pictures of you enjoying them. If you have a deep passion for anything be sure to include a picture that establishes that, however mundane. You may think that nobody would give a shit about your love of pre-Columbian civilizations from the tropical lowlands of south-central Mexico, but throw a photo up of you visiting a site and you may find someone with the exact same passion messaging you asking questions about it.

If you love travelling, then putting up a picture or two of you abroad is fine. Just understand that "well travelled guy" isn't really an identity. So if you are going to put travel pictures up, make sure they say something more than just "I traveled here." If you have a photo of you surfing at Bondi beach in Sydney, then throw that up, but if you have a picture of you simply in front of the Eiffel tower with a goofy smile, then best to leave that one out. Just try to think what else the picture is communicating other than well travelled. Are you in a museum? Are you doing something adventurous? If your picture tells a story and raises questions about who you are, then it's a good picture. It also provides a very easy excuse for the women to message you about it.

You may want to have a picture up that communicates your job as well, depending on what exactly it is. Your profession is a huge part of your identity and if you're lucky enough to have an exciting or attractive profession then be sure to include a photo of you that communicates it. If your job isn't too exciting, let's say you work in an office, then you may want to put up some photos that communicate some of your skills instead. If you've taken first aid, sailing lessons, or survival training, throw a picture up of you that communicates that.

Having pictures that communicate your personality is also something that you'll want. Humour is probably the most important since it goes well with the "I'm not taking this seriously" attitude that you want your profile to reek of. A friend of mine had a professional photo of him with his cat that was taken in a cheap department store and looked hilarious. They were both wearing sweaters. He got messages all the time from women telling him it was hilarious. Try to find a picture that communicates that "I don't give a shit" mentality.

So that should round up all your pictures. Take a look at them and try to think about how you come across when they're taken in as a set. I'd even recommend asking some female friends or even messaging women outside of your city on the dating site itself and ask them what they think your pictures say about you. You can get some great feedback from women when they know your only intention is an honest opinion. Be sure to experiment around as well, and pay attention to how many page views and messages you're getting when you have certain pictures up.

The About Me Section

Every dating site is going to have an "about me" section. It's essentially an opportunity for you to describe and sell yourself in your own words. It's also the most important part of your profile next to your pictures so it's worth putting a lot of thought into how exactly you'd like your potential dates to see you. I'm going to go over a lot of fundamentals as well as some specific tips, but just like everything else, try experimenting with different things. Generally speaking, women's taste in men differs from culture to culture and even city to city in some cases, so you may find that talking about your love of roughing it outside and being adventurous would sound a lot more attractive in a city like Seattle than it would in a city like Los Angeles. Keep that in mind!

Just like your pictures, your "about me" is going to paint a picture of who you are. Understand that when women are reading your profile they're trying to find facts and characteristics of what type of guy you are so they can paint an accurate picture in their head. You're essentially in control of that picture, but there are some not-so-obvious pitfalls and ways that you can fuck it up easily. First of all, your identity of who you are has to be congruent with your pictures; what you put in words should match what you've put in images. This is very important and is going to be the first place a woman will look for congruency. If you make yourself out to be someone spontaneous, funny and artistic in your "about me," but your pictures tell a different story, then ultimately you're going to look like a charlatan. Your "about me" should reinforce your pictures, not question them.

One of the biggest things guys have trouble with when they're trying to sell themselves is bragging. Bragging is something that can be a little tricky when it comes to dating sites because even though you want to communicate your strengths, you also don't want to come across overly-arrogant or, even worse: that you're a try-hard. So how do we communicate our strengths without appearing arrogant or try hard? Easy, it's just a matter of changing a few things about what you're actually trying to communicate with your profile. Instead of thinking "What will women find attractive about me?" you should be thinking "What do women want in a guy, and how can I communicate that I have those things?" That's a slightly different mentality and communicates some social intelligence. Let's go over some qualities that men like boasting about as well as qualities that nearly all women are looking for and how to communicate them in a way that doesn't come across try-hard or overly arrogant.

Money is usually the first thing that men want to communicate with women. Women don't necessarily care as much as men do about this; sure there are plenty of gold-digging women out there but I've found that most women only care about money as far as your ability to provide rather than your ability to pamper. Still, we want to paint ourselves in the best possible light without lying outright so let's talk about how to communicate... well let's call it "success-fulness." Right off the bat, don't bother listing or alluding to how much money you make, even if it's damn impressive. A lot of sites will have an option to list what your salary is, but I'd recommend leaving that blank or choosing any sort of "not willing to disclose" option. Rich men don't need to tell people they're rich, and women know this. It's much better to communicate it with your profile through stories or statements that hint at it. So, for instance, writing in your profile "I'm quite spontaneous, I'm the guy who will decide to randomly take off to the Caribbean for a week on a day's notice and gorge on seafood while getting into as many adventures as I possibly can" communicates that you probably have the resources to do so regularly. It also communicates a lot more than just "I'm rich" since it shows them a bit of your personality. As a general rule, it's much better to gift wrap your braggy bits with personality and character traits to make them a lot more presentable. Also remember what I said about the congruency between your pictures and "about me" section: If you're communicating that you're successful make sure to include a picture or two that proves that. Sometimes this can be as easy as a photo of you wearing a nice suit or having dinner or drinks in a nice venue.

Intelligence is another quality that most men would like to communicate with their profile. Intelligence can also be tricky since it's often relative to what you're looking for. You wouldn't necessarily want to communicate that you're a genius even if you are since it could potentially turn a lot of women off. I believe in communicating intelligence in more covert ways, in ways that only an intelligent woman would potentially recognize. The easiest way to do this without explicitly saying anything is to have good grammar. As popular as internet acronyms are for streamlining what you're saying, I would strongly advise against using them in your profile, especially if you're above the age of 18. There are quite a few women out there who value intelligence enough that they will instantly next you if your grammar is bad. There are an equal number of women out there who will instantly find you a lot more attractive if you have flawless grammar. I advise making sure your spell check is turned on and would even advise having someone who has good grammar take a second look at your profile to see if there's anything you missed. Sometimes something as simple as using a semicolon properly can be enough to warrant a message from grammar-Nazi hotties; seriously it has happened to me numerous times.

Another easy way to communicate intelligence is to mention any interests you have that would reinforce your intellect. Love art, books, music, philosophy, quantum physics? Mention the books, films, compositions, seminars and essays that you particularly enjoy. It may go over most people's heads, but if someone does pick it up, it could be the determining factor if she messages you or not. As well, most people will admire others who are passionate about something regardless if they understand it or not. In fact, passion is something that is worth getting into more detail about...

Communicating your passion isn't as simple as stating what you love. It's about communicating why you love it, and even then you want to almost teach them something about your passion. Personally, I love collecting vinyl records and often explicitly state that in my online dating profile. I don't simply say "I'm a huge vinyl record nerd, I have over 1000 vinyls." That doesn't really help communicate my passion to them. If I said something like "I collect vinyl records, and I personally believe that vinyl sounds better than digital. It just sounds more real." that's better, and may even get me some messages from other women who like vinyl. But that's probably it since again, it's only saying what my passion is with a personal belief as to why, without really explaining anything. So how would I communicate my passion in the best way? Like this:

"I'm really into collecting vinyl records. It's kind of silly, but most of my favourite bands are older and there's something about being able to put a record on the turntable and listen to some of my favourite bands in the exact same way that it would have been played when it was released. It gives me nostalgia for a time period I never existed in."

This gives them a glimpse into my mind. It lets them see my passion the way that I see it, and with my own words. You can do this for anything, even incredibly geeky or juvenile passions. It can require a bit of looking inwards to figure out where your passion comes from, but it's essentially stating your true reasons for your passions. I also really love collecting old video games. I probably wouldn't really ever put that in my profile since I have more important passions I'd like to communicate, but if I did I would say something like:

"I have a huge collection of vintage video games. I don't play them too much, but I have them because my parents never had much money growing up and I never got them all those Christmases ago. As a kid I always promised myself that I would get them someday, so now whenever I look at them that little kid version of me on Christmas morning always smiles back at me."

Wow, isn't that sweet? Now, if I can make collecting video games sound interesting then it shouldn't be too hard for you to do the same for even your most embarrassing passions... unless it's tentacle porn or something.

In order to make your profile, and thus yourself, sound more appealing you may want to specifically address common gripes that women have with meeting guys, especially guys they meet online. There are numerous gripes, but a few stand out and are a lot more all-encompassing. One of the first things women will wonder, if your profile appeals to them, is:

"If I meet this guy would it be awkward or weird?"

This question is basically what determines if a woman will progress at all with the interaction, whether it's messaging you, giving you her number, or finally: meeting up with you. You want to nip this in the bud as soon as possible. I've seen countless women reject what would appear to be awesome guys just because they got a sense of them being shy or awkward. A little timidness or shyness can be excusable in real life, but on the internet women are a lot more selective, mostly because they can be, but also because the internet has a greater concentration of weirdos. One way you can address this gripe is to bring it out into the open. On my "about me" I wrote the following:

"If we hang out there will never be an "awkward silence" so don't worry. If you're nervous, I will just tease you."

Believe me, any woman that has tried the online dating game and met up with more than a couple people has had this happen to her and she HATES it. As soon as they read that if they meet up with you there won't be any awkward moments they're going to breathe a sigh of relief. It may not completely convince them, but couple it with your messages and your phone call that will come later (which I'll be getting into) and it should be enough to convince them that awkwardness will not be a concern.

One thing you can do to quell another gripe that would realistically only come up later on is to demonstrate your lack of fear when it comes to making the first move. Any woman who is considering going on a date with you is also considering having something happen, whether it simply be a kiss or otherwise. Being scared and awkward when it comes to that first move is something that can really turn women off. You can show some virility by explicitly stating in your profile that you have no trouble making the first move. Here are a couple lines you can use to demonstrate this:

"I'm a bit of a scoundrel in that I'm very good at understanding when there's good chemistry, and I've never been the one that's scared of making the first move."

"Contrary to popular culture, real men STILL exist."

"I've always been completely compelled by my emotions to engage in risky behaviour. Sometimes this gets me into trouble, often this gets me into fun ;)"

"Dates shouldn't be awkward, they should be hilarious... and maybe sexy."

This is going to communicate that not only do you have BALLS, but that you're also probably someone who often gets in opportunities to make a move, and that you're usually successful. It's only guys that have bad or no experience that would be awkward in such a situation. It may seem a little presumptuous to talk about this explicitly in your profile, but I've gotten a number of messages from women who told me that they messaged me exactly for that reason. You have to understand that a lot of guys turn to online dating because they're scared of talking to women in reality, and that these are often the same guys that are scared to make a move, even when they have green lights, so you're making yourself stand out from these guys quite dramatically by matter-of-factually stating that it will never happen. She's also been on enough dates to find the quality refreshing as well (unless she's very young, but even then). Just make sure it DOESN'T happen when you go on the date though, otherwise she'll doubt everything else about you (don't worry, I'll be going over the first date later!).

Another massive gripe that women have with guys is that they're BORING. Boredom kills attraction faster than anything else, so if your "about me" doesn't entertain them then they're almost definitely not going to want to message you. Obviously, the easiest way to combat boredom is humour! You're going to want to stay away from obvious stuff though, so it's best to leave reaction seeking humour at the door. I find the best humour is one which re-affirms your "I'm not taking this seriously" attitude. Humour is one of those things that's incredibly difficult to teach, but I'll give you a few examples of how I incorporated it into my profile.

A lot of dating sites have a section of your profile where you can list your interests, and this can be a great place to incorporate some humour. If you have any odd interests you'd like women to know about then you should definitely list them here. If you'd rather make up a bunch of silly interests, you can do that too! I would list things like: Murdering bears, acrobatic assault manoeuvres, living on the edge, rewinding my DVDs, TV/VCR repair, riding moose like horses, laughing maniacally then jumping off bridges, and so on. Not only does it make you seem less needy, but it lets the women know that you have a sense of humour. You can list some actual interests too, but I would put some funny ones in there just for good measure. If you are going to put actual interests in then make sure not to be vague and list interests that would appeal to women.

Another way to incorporate humour is with future adventure projections. Future adventure projections are basically just describing a fantastical situation you are going to experience with her in the future that is a joke. I use these if there's a section for describing your first date as it calls out the fact that actually seriously describing a first date is going to, the majority of the time, sound a little too needy. I did an entire audio interview with Tenmagnet, another Love Systems instructor, about future adventure projections which is available through the Love Systems website if you'd like to know more about them, but I'll include a couple here that I've used for dating sites:

"Let's go to yard sales and collect crappy records then hike up a cliff and throw them into the ocean in an act of defiance. Let's film it and make it a commercial for how awesome we are."

"I'll take you to my secret junkyard where we can build a spaceship out of trash and fly it to another planet with Howie Mandel, like that movie/real life experience I saw when I was a kid/took acid." **This one obviously requires a humorous personality to pull off.**

"We'll dress up as European royalty and have my cat Rod, hereby known as Sir Roderick be our personal squire and introduce us with horns to our table at a mediocre restaurant. I will be Sir Reginald and you will be Lady Evelyn. We will eat crumpets and if things go well maybe have a longing gaze or mild hand holding."

Evoking an Emotional Response

Remember that you want to evoke an **EMOTIONAL** reaction when a woman reads your profile. This is probably the most important element that your profile can have. Let me give you a rundown in the first person of what usually happens when a woman finds a cool guy's profile.

Oh that guy looks cute, let's check out his profile.

Nice pictures, he's definitively not bad looking and he seems cool; let's read his "about me."

Oh, he seems pretty cool, nice too.

Hmm, his profile is well written, and he seems like he's got his shit together...

I kinda like him, maybe I should message him, but what do I write? I don't want to seem desperate... Maybe he'll see that I looked at his profile and message me.

As you can see, what usually happens is that if there's nothing in their profile that gets an immediate emotional reaction from the women, then they won't usually message them. A lot of guys have lots of stuff in their profiles that will get good logical reactions from women (I.E. they're good looking, have a nice job, sense of humour, etc.), but that's often not enough. There needs to be something that will evoke a strong enough response that she will want to message you right then, and the easier the message the better. Most women will not message guys they like. It's the same reason you see the really hot woman with a cool profile, decide you want to message her, spend 5 minutes thinking of what you should send, and then ultimately give up. Women are usually even quicker to give up than we are when it comes to trying to think of a message, so anything in your profile that can evoke enough of an emotional response to have her message you right then is going to be top priority.

So what are some ways in which we can evoke a strong emotional reaction? One of the easiest ways to tell is to look at the messages that women are sending you; often the triggers will be referenced in the messages themselves. It's different with everyone, but there are some things that can be applied across the board. For instance, with my profile I often get messages based on either the imagery I described or from my general sense of cockiness about the whole thing. Actually, I get a lot of messages that simply say "You're a cocky asshole" or "You sound pretty full of yourself." These tend to either be from really hot or morbidly obese women (I'm not sure about the disparity there) but felt it worth noting. In any case, the messages you receive will rarely hint at any sort of attraction on their part, and with good reason: if a woman is willing to message you, she probably doesn't want you to think it's because she was desperate. Let's go over some different emotional triggers we can evoke and how to deal with the responses.

Fantasy Fulfillment

These work well with most women. They're kind of like a future adventure projection but are a little more steeped in reality. In my profile I use a couple, I talk about living on a sailboat exploring the coast and writing, as well as living in a tree house on a tropical island. A lot of women will read something like that, think "That sounds awesome! I would love to do that!" and then message me telling me so. The easiest way to think of these is to ask yourself "If I had all the money I could ever need, what would I be doing with my life?" The answer to that question will be a fantasy you can describe; just remember to concentrate on the experience rather than the luxury and try to keep it modest or at least funny.

How to respond: Play along with the fantasy for a message or two, but then drop it. Much like an opener or chat-up line, talking about a fantasy is a great way to start a conversation, but it needs to go somewhere else if you plan on continuing. Don't milk it too much, although I usually keep the first two messages or so in line with the fantasy:

(This is from an actual chain of messages)

[Her]: OMG I would LOVE to live in the Caribbean, that's also been my dream since I was a kid.

[Cajun]: Hmm I may consider taking you along, how are your pirating skills? Do you know how to train monkeys? Will you wear a coconut bra to boost morale?

[Her]: Lol, yeah I can totally train monkeys as long as they don't throw poop at me. Coconut bra lol I like your thinking.

[Cajun]: I suppose I can bring you along then. Hmm I'll need a full assessment though, actually we should discuss this right now over telephone wire as we'll only have tin cans and twine on the island. May as well get used to it, what's your number, I'll give you a ring in... 10 mins?

> ***Notice how I subtly made the question about when I could call, as opposed to if I could call.***

[Her]: haha you work quickly! Yeah I'll be here in 10, (number). Talk to you soon cutie!

Once on the phone, you don't need to bring up the fantasy much, if at all. Simply use it as something to leap off of.

Commonality

These are the easiest to include and often don't require much thought or creativity to pull off. The trick here is to evoke an emotional response not from the commonality itself (although you can do that if it's obscure enough) but from your personal feeling of the commonality. So instead of saying "Led Zeppelin is the best band ever!" you could say "Led Zeppelin is the best band and babe I'm gonna leave you is their best song.

If you disagree... you are wrong, and I can tell you why." This should prompt an immediate reaction out of her if she has enough interest in the commonality.

How to respond: The big trap here is either continuing to talk about said commonality or grasping at other potential commonalities in an effort to impress her. Your best bet here is to make an observation about her that stems from your common interest. Women are always secretly wondering what their interests say about them; peruse women's magazines at a grocery store and you'll see what I mean. So a good response could be:

> [Her]: *Babe I'm gonna leave you? Really? You can't beat Since I've been loving you.*

> [Cajun]: *Since I've been loving you? Impressive, it's a harder equivalent. Let me guess, you prefer leather over lace, and whisky over wine? You should come throw some Neil Diamond records off a cliff with me...*

> [Her]: *Defs a leather over lace kinda girl, whisky... not so much. Fuck I HATE Neil Diamond, I'm soooo in!*

> [Cajun]: *Alright, I'm making a list of worthy projectiles to keep him shattered company, you should help me decide, what's your number? Let's talk like we're not secretly geeks hiding behind computers.*

> ***Notice how I frame her as nerdy if she refuses to give me her number***

Negative Reaction

Sometimes there will be something in your profile that will elicit a negative reaction from the women reading it. Try not to take this too seriously, as it's much easier for a woman to simply ignore you than to send you a message telling you how much she hated what you said. In fact, in the majority of cases they only do so either in jest or in order to see if you'll stand up for yourself. I get plenty of women messaging me telling me how I'm cocky, an asshole, or straight up full of myself. It's fine, and just like in real life: it's a sign of attraction. It all comes down to how you deal with it. I've always said it's much easier to get a woman to go from hating you to being attracted to you than it is to go from being indifferent to being attracted.

How to respond: Don't bother trying to argue with her, unless it's evident she's simply playing along with something silly you said. Instead, try to subtly coerce her into realizing how ridiculous arguing over a dating site is. As well, never apologize or bend in any way to her negative comments. If anything you should attempt to irritate her further while maintaining an air of jest about the fact that she's even bringing it up. The best way to do this is to play along with her negativity to see how she escalates it.

[Olivia]: Yeah you kind of seem like an asshole...

[Cajun]: I am an asshole.

[Olivia]: Evidently... .

[Cajun]: You talk a lot for someone who doesn't say anything.

[Olivia]: Haha I'm seriously wondering why I keep responding to your messages.

[Cajun]: Probably has something to do with my moustache. Hmm, I'm thinking me and you would never get along, but now I'm curious how fun it would be to fight with you...

[Olivia]: Not much of a fighter, but I make up for it with my mouth.

[Cajun]: Should be great make-up sex then.

[Olivia]: Hahah clever.

[Cajun]: You around tonight? I'm bored, give me your number.

[Olivia]: Just like that huh?

[Cajun]: Yup, I'll even be polite, but only on the phone.

[Olivia]: You really ARE an asshole, haha ok deal, ###-####.

Chapter 2 Messages

Alright, so let's say you find an amazing woman while you're perusing women's profiles on the dating site and want to message her instead of hoping that she messages you. That's fair, there are plenty of attractive women out there who refuse to make the first move, and odds are the ones you really want aren't going to message you. So let's go over some stock openers you can use.

Stock Openers

I'll give you some examples of messages I have used in the past for initiating contact; some of them work better than others. Often it depends on the personality, sense of humour or intelligence of the woman, but I try to screen for that anyway. You'll notice that the openers all tend to follow the same theme of "I'm not taking this too seriously." I've already mentioned (and will continue to do so) why this is so important, but it's especially important here. Understand that most of the messages women receive on dating sites fall into a few categories. In researching this book I've actually set up fake female accounts so I could see the kinds of messages that guys send to women who they're interested in. I'll quickly go over them in case you're interested in order to find out which category your past messages have probably put you into:

IDIOTS: These messages are actually the most common and are probably the main reason many women get frustrated with dating sites and perpetuate the stigma that it's full of creeps. These are often incredibly short messages which offer nothing other than an invitation for the woman to respond back I.E. "wat up gurl?" and "ur seksi" or the ever popular "daaaaaaaaaaaaaaamn." Don't get me wrong, I'm sure women love getting these messages to pet their ego, but don't expect anything more than a polite "thanks!" if any response at all. This category also includes messages that are threatening, sexual or just plain disturbing.

TRY HARDS: These messages often come across as being a little fake or scripted. Often they'll list the obvious commonalities, how much they also love whatever that person loves and basically just reek of neediness:

> *"Oh wow you like Firefly too? I LOVE that show. You live in Riverdale? ME TOO, where do you go? We should get together sometime! Add me on IM desperatechode@foreveralone.com."*

NICE GUYS: These messages are fine in their own right, they just don't communicate anything. A woman may smile and feel validated by them but rarely will they put in the effort to respond back unless they're feeling desperate.

> *"Hello there, I read your profile and couldn't help smiling as I read about your hobbies. You seem very interesting! You seem like someone I'd like to get to know better, tell me more about yourself... "*

ASSHOLES: These guys are few and far between, and in fact probably have the most success with online dating sites. They tend to open with a joke, nonsensical observation, or even an insult. The problem with assholes is that although they may attract plenty of women, they tend to offend just as many, and the ones they do attract often become bored of the act before these guys actually get to the point of meeting them. A good friend of mine does this style and although he often gets dates, dirty pictures and plenty of IM mates from it, he also spends significantly more time doing so.

"You look like a cabbage."

Here are some messages I have used in the past that have worked for me:

"Hey I was thinking of robbing a bank, fleeing down to the oceanfront, driving off a cliff, and faking my own death this week (SCUBA tanks in trunk), are you in?"

"You're pretty much the only woman I've seen on this site who doesn't creep the living hell out of me. Do you like egg salad sandwiches?"

"If you're still looking for your soul mate on this site I just saw two different profiles of guys who live in RVs!! Seriously though have you met anyone on here who is actually normal?"

"I was bored tonight and was clicking on profiles of people and comparing them to vegetables. You reminded me of a coconut, which is my favourite vegetable. This is obviously a compliment since coconuts are amazing, you should come climb trees and find some with me."

This one is obviously a bit nonsensical since I doubt anyone would believe a coconut is a vegetable. It shows some character by incorporating a bit of teasing humour.

> *"You're adorable. I'm adopting you as my little sister so we can drink kool-aid and climb trees. Afterwards we can star in a commercial about how awesome adoption is and you can give a really sad face to the camera but then I come around the corner with a pitcher of kool-aid and your smile turns into a party."*

If she lists any traits that she hates in guys, for instance: "If you have back hair, like Prince or are short, don't bother messaging me." claim that you have all of those amazing traits, so:

> *"Hey I love shaving my back while listening to Prince in my height adjusted platform shoes. I didn't read your profile or anything, but I think we would get along."*

These can backfire sometimes but are almost always worth it for the hilarity.

If she has any interests in her profile that you have in common or that you can comment on, that can make a good message as long as it's not simply stating the commonality and milking it. So instead of sending "Oh man! I love the Clash too, what's your favourite album?" you should try to evoke an emotional response by saying something like "How can you like the Clash and not the Ramones! That's blasphemy!"

If she lists any interests that you could make fun of her for, that can work well too. Just make sure it's playful and not something obvious or too insulting. So something like "Hey I love bingo too! When I'm not doing crosswords and yelling at young people for being too noisy I love playing bingo! Ha ha seriously though? Bingo?" works a lot better than "Bingo? You probably smell like my grandmother's farts. BINGO!"

Dropping the Act

Although playing around and teasing is encouraged for the first couple messages, eventually you have to give in and treat the interaction a little more seriously. This is usually the most ideal time to escalate to a new medium (digital or otherwise) if you haven't already done so. If you continue the act too long there's a good chance she will lose interest. You can always go back to light teasing and cocky banter when you get her off the site and onto IM or the phone.

This gives off the not-so-subtle impression that if she wants to see where this interaction will go she needs to comply and give you her Facebook, IM, or phone number.

> *"Ha ha, you're pretty cute, and playing email tag on an internet dating site is a pretty lame form of communication, give me your number and I'll give you a call in a bit, the funniest thing happened at the grocery store earlier and I need to tell someone, you going to be around later tonight?"*

A message like this does a number of different things:

> *You imply that she could be perceived as lame if she disagrees with you.*

Instead of asking, you assume she's going to give you her number, implying that you most likely do not get rejected often.

The compliment you give her "you're pretty cute" sets the tone that she has won you over only slightly, and you are giving her the privilege of allowing the interaction to go to a more personal medium (in this case phone).

You provide a topic of conversation that the phone call can be based around, in this case your trip to the grocery store (although it can be anything). This way she already knows that she won't be the one having to keep the talk from going awkwardly silent right off the bat.

Once she agrees, it's time to escalate things to the phone, and standard phone game rules apply. There's a chapter later on in the book for the first phone call, but for a much more in depth look at phone game, check out Braddock's Ultimate Guide to Text and Phone Game.

Questionnaire

Some websites use questionnaires to help match you with women in your area. I've spoken with several women about these trying to find out what sorts of answers stick out. What I've found is that most women tend to take these pretty seriously in that they're usually quite honest, so I would not advise goofing around on these as much as you would on the rest of your profile or you're risking not being matched with anybody.

On some sites women can send you a questionnaire as a probe. These usually consist of several multiple choice questions of her choosing, which you of course must answer in order to message her back. There's a bit of a trick with these; I'll show you what I mean:

Your idea of a perfect first date would be?

A. Going for coffee at a cafe.

B. Going to dinner at a fancy restaurant.

C. Cooking a romantic dinner at home.

D. Other: _____.

How would you answer this? **A** seems a bit lame, **B** can leave the wrong impression, and **C** is a bit presumptuous for a first date. The correct answer for this as well as most of the questions you will get will be the last option: "Other." OKCupid and E-Harmony use these questionnaires extensively although I've encountered them with other sites. They almost always give you an "Other" option where you can fill in your own answer. *Always* use the "Other" option as it will give you an opportunity to not only personalize the answer (in the event that there isn't a preferable option) but it also gives you the chance to incorporate some of your wit and charm.

You should be handling the answers to these questions in the same way that you were building your profile: don't take them too seriously. There's no need to go over the top with the answers, often overselling the joke can have the opposite effect and have you come across as needy. Try to keep your answers somewhat short and concise. If the questions tend to be rather serious, for instance "Are you open to children?" or "What are your religious beliefs?" or any other sort of question where you think she may want a serious answer, I would fuck with her a bit for asking, but then answer truthfully. You do not want to appear as if you're dodging anything. Here are some examples of questions I have answered in the past.

"How important is a woman's body when it comes to her attractiveness?"

A: 27.

"How do you feel about dating women older than you?"

A: I had a crush on Blanche from Golden Girls when I was a kid. Any questions?

"How important is religion in your life?"

A. My beliefs about life are very important to me. I do not follow any one religion too closely, but I find beautiful truths in every religion I come across... .except Scientology.

"Your most attractive trait would be?"

A. The circular hurricane pattern that seems to grow in my beard when I haven't shaved in a couple days. Either that or my really awesome cat that can do backflips and other circus magic.

Digital Bouncing

After you've sent a couple messages back and forth through the dating site and received some interest, you may want to start thinking about "bouncing" her to a social networking site. This involves simply convincing her to move the conversation to a more personal medium and can be valuable for a number of reasons:

Most dating sites only allow a handful of pictures to be stored on their site, and often these pictures are not necessarily an accurate depiction of the subject - intentional or otherwise. Adding a woman on a social networking site allows you to get a much more robust set of photos in which to judge her physical appearance.

There are quite a few impostors on dating sites, so adding them on Facebook can add some credibility to their identity.

Important information such as how many friends they have, their personality and how their friends treat them can be obtained.

She can see your page, which will of course be awesome (Don't worry I'll help you with that, read on).

Keep in mind that this is entirely *optional*. If you use a social networking site for personal use with friends and family there are some risks involved: she could stalk you, put inappropriate comments on your page, find out personal info to use against you or many other not-so-fun scenarios. These people do exist so be cautious, take careful note of the privacy settings and make sure not to divulge too much personal info on these sites. I had a woman who I went on some dates with a while back who ended up finding out where I live from Facebook (picture of my house, which she recognized) and then proceeded to show up at my door on drugs at 2am wanting sex. This scenario worked out pretty good since it resulted in sex, but what if she wanted to kill me? You have to think about these things.

Since social networking sites are an entirely different beast, I've decided to devote an entire section to them.

Chapter 3 Social Networking Sites

What I've tried to do in this section is describe how to use social networking sites (namely Facebook) to complement your online dating skills. It is possible to meet women directly from Facebook, but usually only if you're connected to her in some way (mutual friend or otherwise). I will go over some tips on how to do this, but for the most part, Facebook should be used as a bridge to meeting up with a woman or as a way of keeping yourself on the radar of women who may take longer to charm. Ultimately, the most important aspect I'll go over in this section is how to make your profile a great deal more interesting and attractive, which will hopefully help you in all your female pursuits online or otherwise.

Meeting Women on Social Networking Sites

As I previously mentioned, Facebook isn't really designed to help you find single women you haven't met before. This doesn't mean you can't use it for those purposes however. You're going to want to keep in mind a couple of things though:

> *I would advise against messaging random strangers. I'm not even sure how you would search for them, but randomly messaging people who have no friends in common with you*

is going to yield very few if any replies. There are some exceptions though, which I'll go over.

The openers I listed in the previous dating site section won't really work on Facebook since people don't really use it as a dating site. Use the openers I'll provide later.

Don't message every hot female friend of a mutual friend. Very good chance they are going to ask the mutual friend about you, and they'll put two and two together pretty quickly if you're mass messaging their entire female friend list.

Cold Openers

Since Facebook is not a dating site, there's a bit of a trick when it comes to cold opening the women on there. I've really only found a couple of different ways you can do this that work semi-consistently:

Implying That You Already Met Them

This one will work much better if you have mutual friends, since they'll be much more likely to respond warmly. I would simply message them saying:

"Hey I saw that you're also friends with (mutual friend). I'm pretty sure I met you at a party one time. I can't remember which one but your face looks ridiculously familiar, and I think we talked about My Little Pony or something. How do you know (mutual friend)?"

The important thing to note here is that you're not asking her if you really even met her or not, you're just implying that you did and that you had a fun conversation. You can replace "My Little Pony" with something equally childish, although I've found North American women aged 20-30 respond well to that reference. She'll most likely respond back explaining how she knows your mutual friend, and then ask how you know them. Be sure to be honest as she will most definitely talk to the mutual friend about you.

Commenting On Posts They Also Comment On

Again, you can really only do this one if you have mutual friends. When perusing your recent feeds on Facebook, be sure to keep an eye out for posts of your friends that have replies from attractive women. You can reply after them and then call them out. How you do this is up to you, but I find gentle teases, something randomly hilarious or agreeing on obscure points work best. I'll give some examples that I've done:

Corby Tender posted: "Man has anyone ever met an ugly Lauren? What the hell!?"

Hot Lauren: "Nope, we're all gorgeous :)" (Be sure to also *like* her comment here.)

Cajun: "You're god damned right we are!" **High 5 Lauren**"

Hot Lauren: "We? Imposter!"

> *Cajun: "Lauren I just met you and you're already calling me ugly? Sometimes non-Laurens want to feel special too. I got all dressed up after feeling like a hot Lauren and now my mascara is running. I hope you're happy."*

> *Hot Lauren: "LOL"*

Obviously the joke here is that your name is obviously not Lauren and that you're a guy.

> *Dilkin Holmes posted: "Does anyone know something clever to say when women ask you why you don't have a girlfriend?"*

> *Hot Ashley replied: "Just say you're looking for the right woman, or that you're very picky!"*

> *Cajun: "Ashley, everyone knows those lines are bullshit, the correct response is "Because my dick is too big." or "My wife won't let me :("*

> *Hot Ashley: "LOL! Yeah use those!"*

Those are just a couple of examples but how you respond to these will really depend on what the comment posted was. Be sure to *like* her comment as well since she'll be notified of that as well as the fact that you replied to it, which nearly guarantees she will see it. After receiving a strong positive reaction in the form of a reply I would go ahead and try to add her as a friend. If she doesn't reply or *like* your comment then you may want to wait until you've replied to a few of her posts on mutual friends' walls.

Accidental Creeping

These are pretty tricky, and often situational. If you somehow find out a woman's name that you like or think is cute, you can use this one depending on how you figured her name out. I'll give you an example of how this is used.

There was this woman who worked at a coffee place by my house named Kassandra - she was gorgeous! I flirted with her a couple times, but I was always with another woman so I never tried to get her number. I came back a couple times a few weeks later and she wasn't working. I asked the other woman working where she was and she said she quit to work at another shop closer to her place. I didn't want to ask her which place and appear creepy in front of what could be her close friend, so instead, I did a Facebook search for women named Kassandra in Toronto. There were probably 100 or so Kassandras with the parameters I set and I eventually found her profile. I sent her the following message:

> *"Hey, this is probably going to sound a bit creepy but I promise I'm normal. You worked at the coffee shop by my place and we've talked a couple times. You're cute! I was out of the country the past week for work and when I came to get my coffee today they told me you left! This sucks because I wanted to get to know you better. I should have asked for your number but didn't have my phone with me the last time I saw you. So if you'd like, send me your number and I'll give you a call tonight."*
>
> *~Derek*

These really only work in these special circumstances. If she doesn't know who you are, at least remotely, she probably won't add you. These can come in handy when you meet people in public and cannot or did not get their number or even talk to them too much. Examples include parties, the gym, waiting in line at the bank, women working where you go to regularly, etc. It's always better to introduce yourself in person, but when you can't do that, this works well enough.

Chatting

Facebook has a chatting function which I recommend taking advantage of. I'll be talking more about chatting later but it's worth noting here that chatting is really the only way to consistently escalate on Facebook. I'll have logs of my chats later on in the book so you can see what types of dialogue work best.

Staying on Her Radar

Once you have them on Facebook you have a couple options of how to proceed, which really depends on how you met or added them and what their level of interest is.

High Level of Interest

This involves simply trying to get their number as soon as you can, which is often immediately although doing some chatting first on Facebook can make it a bit easier. Simply send them a message through Facebook, or even on the chat, and ask them for their number.

"Hey, thanks for the add! To be honest I don't really use Facebook all that much, I just wanted to stay in touch with you. You around later? Send me your number. I need to tell you the most amazing thing that happened to me today. You won't believe it."

As mentioned previously in the messages section, the story can really be anything; it's just an excuse to get her number.

Low Level of Interest

These can take some time but are often worth waiting for if it's the only option. This strategy follows a series of escalating interactions.

Stay on her radar: Start liking her comments and posts, occasionally reply. Don't over do this, maybe once every couple weeks or so. This may take several weeks.

Become "Facebook friends": This usually involves multiple chats and posting funny replies to her comments. You will know you're here when she initiates chats or posts on your wall.

Interact quite often on Facebook through chats, replies, wall posts. Get her number to relay a funny story. On chat: "Oh man funniest shit ever happened today. I need to tell you this in person. What's your number?"

This whole process may take several weeks or months. Once you have her on the phone, regular phone game rules apply.

Creeping

"Creeping" is the term that is used to describe the act of snooping over someone's profile without his or her knowledge. Let me tell you right now that this type of behaviour is RAMPANT among young women. If you add a woman you met on a dating site to Facebook, you can be sure that she's going to look at nearly EVERYTHING on your profile to find out who you are, and she will jump to conclusions if there's anything there that could be even remotely suspect. Some are worse than others, but it pays to take a tight control over what is being displayed or communicated on your profile.

You can actually use this to your advantage to find out what's working or what's not on your profile. I found that for a while, when I was adding women from dating sites to Facebook, I would lose contact with them. I couldn't understand this until I got a female friend to look at my Facebook profile and tell me what she would think if she didn't know me, and she was able to spot the problem right away. Turns out that most of my pictures had me drinking or holding a drink. So women were, presumably, thinking I was an alcoholic. I never would have suspected this since it just so happened that most pictures of me were usually taken on nights out. I had to go through my photos and clear out all the extra drinking photos and once I did I never had that problem again. Try changing things up or even having a female friend or LS instructor give a second opinion if you're having trouble keeping in contact once you have them on Facebook. Another option is to set up a second Facebook profile strictly for your online dating pursuits. This has its pros and cons: pros being that you can construct your entire profile with dating in mind without spilling any personal information, and cons being that you may have to work at making your friend's list not appear completely made-up.

There are lots of other problems that they could catch from your profile though. **Incriminating photos are one thing, but messages, groups you belong to, and even who you're friends with (depending on the notoriety of said friend) could be deal-killers.** I'm not saying you have to be super paranoid about this stuff, but if there's something on your profile that you think could be taken the wrong way: it probably will be. I had one woman who constantly put overly suggestive comments on my wall, something that can occasionally help (which I'll get into later), but there's a big difference between "It was great seeing you last night!" and "Amazing night, next time you're staying over here with me... " The former is discreet while the latter is pretty blatant, and it caused some problems with some of the other women I was dating that I also had on Facebook. Remember: If women think you're someone with options, that's good, but if it's being thrown right into their face, whether intentional or not, that's bad, and they lose some respect for themselves and you. Being discreet is always to your advantage and remember you can always delete anything on your profile, be it wall posts or even news feeds I.E. "Cajun is now friends with Kitty the townwhore 3:07am," so take ownership and keep a keen eye.

Creeping isn't all pitfalls though, since it can also give you some advantages as well. As I've already mentioned, most people are oblivious to how much information their Facebook profile reveals about them. You can find out hobbies, interests, goals, lifestyle and personality types all from creeping their profile if you so choose. Your ability to see this information will depend on the privacy restrictions that the women set for you, although many women set no restrictions whatsoever. Often, simply searching her name (if you've obtained it) on Facebook will result in unrestricted access to her profile, even if she hasn't added you as a friend! These things can come in handy when you do finally meet her, as you'll already know some things about her that you may have in common (although I wouldn't let on that you found out through Facebook, so you may want to act surprised!). It can also give you some ideas about the types of conversations you can have during the date. I've included the Question Game at the end of this book so that you can have a nice blueprint for the conversation during the date, but throwing in some conversations about commonalities and aspirations or goals will always help. Sometimes something as simple as having read the same book can be a game changer in a date, so be prepared and do your homework!

Avoid posting anything out in public on her wall, so no "Thanks for adding me!" or "Nice to meet you!" As I've mentioned a number of times, women don't want to feel as if they've needed to resort to online dating to meet guys, and when you post on their wall for all the world to see, they're going to start thinking what their friends and family are thinking of and that will most likely make them self-conscious. Keep it discreet, and only send private messages for now.

You may also want to check out her history to see if she's been adding a number of different guys lately. If her wall shows that she has recently become friends with an unusual amount of guys it could give you some clues as to how she's using the internet dating site. Some women just collect guys to pad their Facebook and give them compliments, so check out her photos and see if there's a number of impersonal compliments being thrown her way by guys. Women tend to compliment each other when they're friends, but guys don't usually compliment their female friends in photos unless they want to fuck them. So if there are a bunch of suggestive photos with male comments saying stuff like "Fuck ur sexy girl" and "Damn! You look so hot in this pic!" then you can bet she probably only has those guys around for the compliments, and you may be her new addition. Also make sure that you have her real page and not her fan page. A lot of women scour dating sites to get fans for their "modeling career" Facebook fan page. Same as the previous example; these women do not really want to meet you and are only using you for your +1 and compliments. Don't be a sucker.

It may seem like I'm being overly cautious here with all these warnings, but the real reason you want to add her on Facebook is to make sure that she is a *real, normal* person. There are tons of gorgeous real women on internet dating sites but there are also crazies, men playing women, psychos, and basket cases. So your primary objective when creeping them is to make sure that their page looks legit. Here's a quick list:

Creeping Priorities

Make sure they look like the pictures they showed on the site.

>Like I've already said, women will tend to use the photos that make them look the hottest when they're limited to only a few images. Facebook will most likely have a lot more and give you a better showcase for their physicality. Occasionally you will be pleasantly surprised to find out that they're actually hotter than what they showed on the site, that's always a good sign since down-to-earth women tend to do that.

Check out how many friends they have.

>This will let you know if she's wildly popular or a recluse. Neither extreme is necessarily good or bad; it really comes down to the type of woman you want. If she has less than a hundred friends, depending on the size of the town, that could be weird. Likewise if she has thousands, that could also be weird. There are normal exceptions to either case though, so don't judge too quickly. Some people don't use Facebook that much and others simply add whoever they meet in life and don't take the site too personally. We're only looking for clues here so don't jump to conclusions.

Look at their info.

>Lots of good intel can be obtained here. Their job, religion, interests, relationship history etc. As I mentioned earlier, take careful note of any commonalities for later use.

Look at their wall.

>What is posted on their wall and how their friends talk to them can give you some clues into the type of person they are. It can also let you know what she finds interesting or funny based on what she posts on her wall.

Some Final Thoughts

Don't make a big deal out of getting them on Facebook; it's just one step closer to meeting her and it doesn't count for much until then. If they take it seriously by referencing things about you that they got from it, teasingly make fun of them. Never bring up info you got from it. Act as if you didn't even look, and file away the knowledge as if everything you found out happened naturally. Your mindset here is that you didn't add them on Facebook because you want to be their Facebook buddy; it's that it's just less "creepy" communicating through a social networking site than it is on a dating site.

So now you've creeped her profile page enough that you have a pretty good idea of who she is and you're fairly certain she's a real, normal person, awesome! Well guess what? She just did the exact same thing to you. Before I even mention how to escalate further I want to make sure that her experience viewing *your* page was just as satisfying. Since I want this book to basically guarantee you to get laid, I feel that it's important that I go through how to set up your Facebook profile with just as much detail as I did in your online dating profile.

Chapter 4: Breaking Down Your Facebook Page

Congratulations, you've garnered enough interest from a woman that she has added you to Facebook. Hooray! Don't get too excited though, because your Facebook could be what makes or breaks you as a potential for her. Remember all those things I mentioned earlier that you would want to pay close attention to on *her* Facebook? Well she's going to be doing the exact same thing to *your* page, except she'll most likely be twice as thorough and half as forgiving. No sense worrying about it, so let's get down to brass tacks and get your page in tip-top shape before you ruin any more opportunities.

Since there are so many tips and tricks you can use to your advantage on Facebook, I'm going to get pretty detailed in this section. Normally, if this were a seminar or a video I would never do this as I would probably lose you in the details, but since this is a book, you can read it over and over, so I'm going to get as detailed as I can. Take this stuff incrementally; don't try to tackle it all at once or you'll get overwhelmed. Making your Facebook awesome may take months, or even years, so this may be a section you come back to again and again. I've spent *years* making my Facebook page as conducive to attracting women as I can, so everything in this section is a product of many years of trial and error.

Alright, so just like your online dating profile, the first thing she's going to look at is your pictures. In Facebook your pictures are a lot more complicated than they are in your online dating profile because you have so much more to work with. She will almost assuredly look at nearly every photo you have unless it's in the thousands, so every one counts. The good thing about Facebook is that it lets you group the photos according to how it made it onto your page. There are profile pics, tagged photos, and albums, and I'm going to get into each of these individually.

Profile Pictures

Much like your dating profile, these are the first pictures she will see. There's your main picture that shows up when you search your name and then every other picture that you've designated as your profile picture at some point in the past. This is an album that has lower security restrictions than your other albums so it's the most important as she will almost assuredly see all these pictures no matter what level of restriction you allow her access to on your profile.

Your main picture is the picture that will define who you are when she finds your profile through the search, so it's a good idea to make this one stand out, just like you did in your dating profile. All the same advice I gave you about your online dating profile picture would apply here, but you have a little more to work with on Facebook since your profile pic isn't necessarily your only opportunity to win her over. This means that although you can get away with having pictures that are more reflective of your personality than your looks, I wouldn't have an ugly or embarrassing (no matter how funny) photo serving as your profile pic. Think about what she'll think of who you are when she sees your profile picture. Are you the butt of all your friends' jokes? Or are you a cool guy with lots of friends who respect him? Your profile picture can communicate these things.

If you have a common name you're definitely going to want to either personalize your name a bit to stand out from the others (most of the time simply adding an initial can solve it) or have something on your profile photo to make it recognizable with only a short description. I actually used my same "pirate" picture I used on my dating site profile so that I could simply say "I'm the one with the eye-patch" when women searched for me on Facebook. It doesn't even have to be anything that clever, just as long as it's immediately recognizable with your description. This may not seem like anything too important for some of you, but if you've ever had to wade through pages of results carefully inspecting the pics to make sure it was the same person you saw on the site, then you'll understand. Most women have a hair-trigger when it comes to "nexting" guys off dating sites, so you don't want your common name and hard-to-find-profile be what causes her to give up on you. Facebook now even has an option to add a custom URL that links to your personal Facebook page; this can make things much easier since instead of her trying to search for you, you can say "Add me on Facebook,

www.Facebook.com/cajunthelegend."

I usually like to have a profile picture that features me either entertaining or winning the admiration of my friends, with at least one female present. I will look for photos where I look like I am hosting whatever events are taking place and people are happy to be in a picture with me. That may sound a little obtuse but look through your photos and try to find one where you look extremely confident or the centre of attention. Pictures that communicate your personality or lifestyle are also useful here.

Here are some of the photos I've used in the past to give you an idea:

Tagged Photos

Tagged pictures work a little differently. They're pictures that show up under your profile photo and are automatically added whenever somebody tags you in a photo. The problem with tagged photos is that you have somewhat less control over them than your profile pictures since any of your friends could tag you in a photo without your approval. You can always UN-tag yourself later, but depending on how often you log in to Facebook, sometimes the damage is already done. Make a pact with your friends when you're out with them that any embarrassing photos will not be tagged on Facebook! If your friends are anything like mine however, you may still awake to find those photos of you puking on a dog all over your front page. Just un-tag and hope nobody saw them for now. If the problem persists you may want to re-evaluate your friends, or at the very least, alter their permissions so they can't tag you in photos.

There are certain types of pictures that you're always going to want to un-tag yourself in. Much like your dating profile photos, any photos where you look like you're hitting on women should be hidden or filed away in an album. You may think that that photo of you making out with the hot blonde at the club makes you look awesome, but all it really says is that you felt the need to broadcast it to all your friends, which really communicates insecurity and lack of pre-selection. If the women are hitting on you, that's good, so anything involving you in a relaxed position with women hanging off will work quite nicely.

Albums

Album photos are photos that are arranged in sets and don't usually contain tags. These are usually the last set of photos that women will look at but are still quite important. This is usually the order women will follow when perusing your profile:

> *Check out profile pics.*
> *Check out tagged pics.*
> *Check out wall, look at friends.*
> *Check out albums.*

Of course it doesn't always follow this order, but that's generally how the flow works. The idea here is that your album photos should give them some information that your tagged photos do not or cannot. What I mean by that is you can communicate more with your albums depending on how willing she is to snoop through them. It's entirely up to her how much she wants to learn about you. The types of photos you should be putting here are things like trips, childhood photos, events or nights out in your past, accomplishment photos or any other types of "braggy" photos. Your album photos will simply paint a much more well-rounded identity of who you are. Obviously the more women know about who you are, the more comfortable they will become with you. This makes escalating to the phone or a date much easier.

Friends

Your friends can actually say a lot about you. Guys won't usually pay much attention to a woman's friends on Facebook other than the number of friends she has. Women look at the number of friends you have as well, but they also tend to look at your actual friend lists. Is it mostly guys with a few ugly women peppered in? That will raise some red flags. What about who your actual friends are? This can be especially troublesome in small towns if your best friends are the *who's who* of the local tabletop RPG scene. I'm not saying you have to change your friends, but you do want to at least give the *illusion* that you have options. Let's go over how to do that.

So your first step is to actually start making new (female) friends. This is actually easier than it sounds, especially for online friends. Whenever I'm out at bars, or even in the daytime and talking to a woman for more than five to ten minutes (see Love Systems' Daytime Dating eBook!) I'll usually add them on Facebook. It's not hard to get someone's Facebook add after only conversing for a little while. Just be nonchalant about it:

> *[Cajun]: You're pretty cool, you sticking around for a while?*

> *[Woman]: Yeah, I think, we may head over to the king's head later.*

> *[Cajun]: Alright, well I'm ignoring my friends so I have to get back to them, but here let me add you on Facebook so we can keep in touch if I don't see you again tonight. *pull out phone**

Just like getting a number, you want to pull out your phone as if it's assumed she will give you the information. Obviously having a smartphone makes adding each other to Facebook even easier since you can do it instantly, so you may want to invest in one. Some women use Facebook for very personal reasons (keep in contact with family and close friends), so don't necessarily take a denial to be added on Facebook as a flat out rejection. It's usually because she doesn't want her nosey aunt keeping tabs on all the new boys she meets. Tell her you understand. You can even mention that you have nosey family on there too, then get her number and tell her you'll text her later. You can always add her later once she feels more comfortable with you.

You can also use the excuse of inviting her to an event to get her Facebook. A cool show, a friend's band, an interesting venue she's never been to, or even a house party are all acceptable reasons to get her Facebook add. The point here isn't really to even get her to come to the event, it's simply to get her Facebook add. Hell I've even made events up completely when there was nothing cool happening in the immediate future. These events work better when they're at least mildly related to the conversation you had with her. So don't go inviting her to the Neil Diamond karaoke showdown if you just talked about your mutual love for early Black Sabbath - actually that might be pretty funny...

Now, once you've got her on Facebook it's time to milk her for what we call social proof - essentially a way of communicating to other women that you have women attracted to you regularly. I'll usually send a message on her wall the next day as a way to bait her into putting one on mine. Don't think too hard about the message. It can be an inside joke, a re-invitation to the event you mentioned, or simply a light tease. The ever popular "Nice meeting you last night!" can work, but I tend to avoid it because then it paints you as "The guy she met last night" to all her friends. "Hey nice running into you last night, had a great time" works a bit better since it implies you may have already known her, but if her wall shows that she just became friends with you right under it, it's still painting you as that guy. You also want something that will elicit enough of an emotional reaction that she'll want to reply to your post. Here are some that I have used in the past:

> *"Hey I won the dairy challenge last night. I look forward to your support in the finals."* **(Inside joke)**

> *"The concert is friday, not saturday. Wear your best bloody t-shirt! If you need some blood let me know."* **(Re-invitation)**

> *"Your profile picture gave me a craving to make pancakes and watch gremlins. You're only allowed to take this as a compliment."* **(Tease)**

All of these messages stirred up enough emotions in them that they posted back on my wall. Things like "Haha name the time and the place," "Yes, I will definitely need some of your blood," and "How could I NOT take that as a compliment!?" To any woman looking at my wall, these messages are very telling. They make me sound like someone who has options, which is exactly what you want them to think.

These woman whom you're befriending should be used for social proof, but don't think you can't converse with them outside of Facebook. It's worth making legitimate friends with these women even if you have no interest in them sexually because it'll help you meet other women and give you women you can invite out to events in order to increase your social proof when you DO leave the internet. You may want to keep some of the women you end up meeting from the dating sites themselves on your Facebook to be used for social proof purposes. I remained friendly with a number of women that I ended up going on dates with and used them to keep my Facebook looking pimp. Whether you want to keep them as simply friends or friends with benefits is up to you.

Chatting

Facebook has a chatting application included and it has its uses. It's probably better in the long run to simply try and get her phone number, either from the dating site or Facebook itself, and call her if you think you have enough attraction to do so. If she's still wary of you however, it may be better to charm her a bit more with the Facebook chat. This is fine but a little unreliable since you don't want to wait around until she's online so you can chat with her. I've included quite a few pages of chat logs in the logs section so you can get an idea of the types of things you can talk about in order to get her more comfortable with you. There are also some great examples of escalation in those as well.

As a general rule for Facebook chatting specifically though, if she's online while you are on, then go ahead and try to get a conversation going; but don't force it, and don't end up writing books. People usually have a tab open to Facebook when they're working, and the constant beeps of new chats can get pretty annoying, especially if the messages are several paragraphs. I'll usually keep my chatting on Facebook limited to short, explosive, funny conversations that I end as soon as they reach a high point. Usually what I imagine amounts to a couple of laughs from her, and then make an excuse (an exciting or fun one!) to leave. You can do this over a couple days, or if she's the type that may take a while to win over, what we call a *long-fuse*, over a couple weeks or months before you end up getting her number.

There are other devoted applications for chatting as well such as Yahoo, MSN, and Skype. I prefer Skype since it seems to be the most popular as well as having a great video chat function. Don't underestimate video chat either; this can often be a great opportunity to build comfort before meeting a woman. Up until she sees you in the flesh, you're still going to be "internet guy" and the video chat can bridge that jump between "random internet guy" and "real person." Obviously make sure your room is clean and you look halfway decent. If she wants to turn video on and you look like shit, simply say you gotta finish something first but you can do it in five minutes, then start cleaning yourself up. Make sure you have a decent angle as well; low angles tend to be unflattering as well as harsh light. Invest in a decent desk lamp with a diffuser and you should be fine.

Some guys I know advocate going sexual during the video chat and trying to escalate enough that the women perform sexual acts such as flashing or strip teases. I have no problem with this once you've already met them in person, but if you haven't, you're most likely going to end up with a woman who, at best, will feel too ashamed to meet you after performing, or at worst, genuinely creeped out by your sexually explicit advances.

Using Skype also has the advantage of being able to make Skype phone calls. This is actually quite useful for a number of reasons:

It's often much easier to escalate to a Skype call if you're already within the Skype chat application. In my experience it's not considered as personal as a phone call. You can also simply send a call invite in mid-chat and type "PICK UP!" and then tease her if she stalls. This often goads them into picking up the call.

If you travel often, using the cheap long distance rates that Skype calls offer can allow you to keep in touch with your prospective women with minimal cost.

Since Skype-to-Skype calls are free, it's also useful if women have low limits on their cell plan and don't want to waste cell minutes on someone they don't really know yet.

Although somewhat rare, if a woman still lives with her parents, and it's late, she may be more inclined to use Skype than risk being caught on the phone (again, this is assuming she can't use her cell for whatever reason).

Chapter 5: Phone Game

By: Tenmagnet

At one point, getting a phone number used to be a big deal. As recently as the early 2000's, a lot of people didn't have caller display, and so getting a woman's phone number usually meant she would actually wind up picking up the phone and talking to you. Sadly those days are past. Phone numbers can still be really valuable, but only if you set the stage properly. Thankfully, when you get a woman's phone number doing online game, you can be pretty sure that she wants to talk to you.

This chapter is going to be about what to do once you have that phone number. How do you move from the phone to a date? If your phone game is good, you should be able to meet up with a woman pretty much every time you get her phone number, but you have to do things right.

There are two things you need to do to cross the bridge from getting a phone number to getting a date. And you have to do them in a particular order.

First, you have to make her **want** to meet up with you. This means moving forward on the *emotional progression* part of the Love Systems triad. You do this by building attraction and comfort in your phone conversations. The most important of these is **comfort**.

Second, you need to **organize the meet up.** This means moving forward on the *logistical progression* part of the Love Systems triad. Organizing the meet up sounds pretty straightforward, but it's actually a stumbling block for a lot of guys, especially because women can be busy, flakey, forgetful or sometimes even playing games with you over the phone. Your skills at organizing the meet up can actually make a big difference in your odds of landing a date with a woman you're interested in, and we'll go into some detail on how to make all that work.

Making Her Want to Meet Up

Usually, when you get a woman's phone number online, she has not yet decided that she wants to go on a date with you, so you can't just move towards arranging a date.

Even if you have been talking about a date and she has been giving you good signals, you still want to presume that there is a bit of work to do on the phone. Oftentimes, one good 10 minute conversation is all that you need, but if you skip this step - if you go straight to **organizing** the date, without first getting her **emotionally ready** to meet up with you - you're going to find a lot of women drop out or flake on you. (I'm going to talk more about flaking later).

First, you should understand where a woman is coming from when she gives you her phone number online. Obviously, there is some attraction there - on an online dating site, women usually won't even respond to a guy if there is no attraction. But there isn't a lot of comfort. If you've been following the method we've given you so far, you've probably only read one another's profiles, seen a few pictures, and chatted back and forth for 2-5 messages.

Essentially, you are still a stranger, probably an attractive one, but still a stranger. And you're a stranger from the internet, no less. And that will make her feel awkward.

Overcoming this awkwardness is the most important thing you **need** to do in your first couple phone calls. And the way you do this is to **build comfort.** Building attraction is not that important at this point, because you already built enough attraction to get her phone number, and you can build a lot of attraction on the date later. Over the phone, **it's comfort that makes a woman want to meet up with you.**

Building Comfort

If you want to learn how to build comfort over the phone, you first need to understand how women see phone conversations.

Men and women view the phone, and communication in general, quite differently. Men, especially men who tend to be analytical, logical and nerdy, tend to want to "get down to business" when they talk on the phone. When guys talk on the phone, they want to teach something, learn something, solve a problem, organize something, and that's about it. The idea of just **sharing** and talking about ourselves seems kind of weird. We feel like a conversation needs a *point* to be worthwhile or interesting.

Women, you may have noticed, don't have a problem sharing and chatting on the phone. They engage in phone conversations that, from many guys' perspective, often seem pointless or superfluous.

But there is a point, it's just not a point that most guys value highly. The point of these apparently superfluous conversations is to cultivate a strong relationship with the person on the other line. Women are constantly talking about their feelings and trying to understand the feelings and perspectives of the people around them, because that's how they form friendships, build comfort, and maintain their social circles. Because of this, *women see an intrinsic value in better understanding the people around them.* Guys have this too, but not really to the same level.

This is what women often mean when they say that they would like a guy to talk about **his feelings.** They're not saying they want to engage you in a therapy session, and talk about all the heavy things that are affecting you emotionally. What "talking about feelings" usually means is talking about yourself in a way that illuminates your character, your values, and the way you see the world.

So, back to the phone conversation. The way you build good comfort in a phone conversation is by sharing a bit about yourself and your personality, and letting her know how you tick a little bit. The big thing that most guys do wrong when they call a woman, especially from an online game situation, is they *try to get down to business too early.* We don't feel comfortable talking about ourselves, or our feelings, so we just go to what we feel comfortable with, which is usually scheduling a meet up, or talking about what we're going to do with a woman. This is all perfectly fine, but you need to **build comfort first**; otherwise, she's going to feel awkward meeting up with you, and women **hate** awkwardness.

The other thing that guys tend to do wrong is they talk about themselves, but they feel like they have to be **really interesting** to keep a woman's attention. The fact is, if a woman is *interested in you* she is *interested in learning more about you.* You can have a conversation with her that would bore the crap out of your guy friends, or that would bore you yourself, and she will be OK with that. That doesn't mean you can be boring, but simply that getting personal and sharing with her will be interesting, so long as there is an initial degree of attraction.

Getting More Specific – Mini Comfort Stories

One of the ways I like to build both comfort and attraction in a phone conversation is by giving a woman a little window into my life on the first call – and making sure that window is showing something good. The way I do this is by telling her a bit about my day – something I've just done, or that I'm about to do. And I just try to make it sound fun, like it's something she would like to do too. You could call these "mini comfort stories."

Let me give you an example of the way I would use a mini comfort story in a conversation. This is an example of a real life story that I used all the time to start off my phone conversations with women I had met on the internet and elsewhere.

> *<Ring>*
>
> *[Tenmagnet]: Hey, it's Chris from PlentyofFish. How's it going?*
>
> *[Her]: Not bad, how are you?*
>
> *[Tenmagnet]: I am actually just coming back from kickboxing class. Have you heard of Muay Thai? <pause... answer doesn't really matter> Well, there's this Muay Thai gym just a few blocks from my house, so I go there every week. It's run by this amazing little thai man who looks kind of like a wooden statue with leather stretched over it, and he's awesome. He makes me work out about ten times harder than I would if I was just going to the gym myself. The classes are 90 minutes long, and I usually want to quit after about 15, but I stick it through and I always feel amazing afterwards. Are you the sporty type?*

Sadly, I moved away and no longer have a convenient Muay Thai Kickboxing gym in my neighborhood, but when I did, it made a fantastic way to open up a phone conversation. Notice how this little story is very natural and relaxed. It doesn't sound like I'm trying to impress her; it's not crazy or wild or attention grabbing. It certainly doesn't sound like a "routine," though you might say it is.

This is a story that works because I **know** she's already into me, and what she wants is to just feel me out a little bit, to make sure I'm a normal guy she can relate to. I'm building attraction subtly by communicating good things about myself: that I'm athletic (the workout), that I'm slightly badass (the Muay Thai), and that I'm a good storyteller (the artsy description of my instructor). But most importantly, I'm communicating that I'm a guy she can relate to, and she can picture what my day to day life is like.

Here's another example, one that's a bit more mundane.

> *[Lauren]: How's it going?*
>
> *[Tenmagnet]: It's going great. I just spent the morning sitting in my favorite café, reading a book and doing a bit of writing. I think it's very important, when you have a beautiful day like today, that you get yourself out of the house and get some fresh air. Also, the cookies they make there are absolutely amazing, what did you get up to?*

All I'm doing in this story is taking a good element of my everyday life and describing it in a way that makes it sound a bit romantic.

So, how do you make your own mini comfort story? It's pretty simple.

First, take something you do in your day to day life that you enjoy or are passionate about. It could be a sport, a creative outlet, an ambition or anything. It doesn't have to be terribly exciting – just something that's hopefully a bit cooler than what she was doing that day.

Then you work on spicing it up. Think about what it is that you like about this activity, and specifically how it makes you feel. A comfort story isn't just a window into your day to day life, it's a window into your values and your mind. So the reason why you do things is often crucially important for creating comfort. Also, remember that women find this stuff a lot more interesting than guys do, so don't be worried if it sounds a bit inane to you. Women will judge you by what the story says about your character, so you want to make sure the character you're conveying is a positive, attractive one. You want to convey, subtly, the Love Systems attraction switches.

Then, you want to give it a nice smooth intro, and an exit. Your story should flow easily from the introduction, and should end with a good comfort question. The way you segue into the story is easy: it's something you are just coming from, or just going to. The exit can just be a regular comfort question that is related to the topic, such as "are you sporty?" or "are you into (whatever I was just talking about)." The comfort conversation that follows will also be important for getting her out.

When Should I Call?

Timing is a very important factor in keeping the momentum up in your interaction with a woman whom you met online. If you wait too long between phone calls, you risk things becoming stale, and the energy starts to fade. Call too often and you come across over-eager and needy. The key is to find a good balance.

Now, you're probably thinking to yourself *how often is a good balance.*

Unfortunately, there's no clear cut answer. Sometimes if you have great chemistry with a woman, you can call her every day; other times, twice a week is plenty. A big part of this is the chemistry and the quality of the conversation between the two of you. As long as you are doing a good job of keeping the conversation going, calling her every two to three days works well.

If I know I'm not going to see her for a few weeks, say it's holiday season, or we're both just really busy, I might reduce that down to once a week. For someone who is from out of town, who I might not see again for several months, I would call once a month to keep the fire warm. But every two or three days is the usual.

But What Do I Say?

How many times have you sat by the phone, wanting to call a woman, and thinking, "I want to call her, but what do I say when I get her on the line?" This question is a source of anxiety to a lot of men, and often they wind up not calling a woman because of this anxiety.

The first thing you need to realize when you have this problem is *you don't have to be an amazing conversationalist to have a good phone conversation.* A lot of guys think they need to be a genius and make a woman laugh like crazy to be good on the phone, but the fact is, the standards are much lower. This isn't television, where every phone conversation has been carefully scripted by expert writers over hours and hours.

Realizing that you don't have to have something brilliant to say in order to have a good phone conversation, just *decide to call her.* Hesitating too long between getting her number and calling her will hurt your momentum and chemistry, and is much worse than simply calling and not having anything particularly clever to say.

And remember: **If she likes YOU, she'll like learning more about you.**

What about Text Messaging?

Text messaging is a great way to communicate, especially late in the game when you're simply trying to organize a meet up. However, text messaging is a very poor way to build comfort – and comfort is one of the most important things you want to be creating when you're on the phone.

So, go ahead and text away, but **don't let texting replace a good, old-fashioned phone conversation.** You really need to have at least a 10 minute phone conversation with a woman to build the comfort required to get her to want to come out. Texting really doesn't cut it, unless you're a fantastic writer.

Organizing the Meetup

Usually, on the first phone conversation that I have with a woman, I won't invite her out. This isn't a hard and fast rule, but simply good practice. It forces you to focus on **comfort building** during the first phone conversation, which is what you should be doing anyways. Also, not inviting her out the first time you call a woman allows a bit of awkwardness to dissipate, and there is often a fair bit of awkwardness going on in the first phone conversation with a woman you met online.

On the second phone call, however, it's time to arrange the meet up.

Chapter 6: Tenmagnet

Online Dating Primer
By: Keychain

Congratulations on investing in this book! Online dating is fantastic and I know of no better man than Cajun to show you the ropes. I've been enthusiastically recommending this area ever since he helped me set up my first profile in early 2010. I was delighted to discover that all of my cold approach and social circle skills were transferable – teasing, text game, escalation, the emotional progression model. In fact, I found the process of contacting and messaging online actually strengthened these very same skills when I took them back into cold approach situations!

Here, in this appendix, is a basic primer on the topic. Although this primer is gleaned from my own online adventures, there should be plenty of overlap with Cajun's material and it's my hope that yet another perspective on the topic might shed even more light for you.

Preparation

First, choose your dating site. Shop around, read reviews, and try discounted trials before signing up to anything long term. I personally favour subscription sites; the interfaces are usually easier to use and I've found the number of genuine, active profiles to be a little higher than on some of the free sites. I know others think differently, so try a bit of everything before settling.

Next, you'll need a good profile. It doesn't have to be perfect, since you'll tweak it over time anyway. Just follow the advice in this book and get something serviceable with some good pictures. After that, it's time to get stuck in!

Your First Message

Dating online, more so than other forms of dating, is in large part a numbers game. With a good profile you may get some unsolicited messages, but if you want to make the most of your subscription you're going to have to send some messages. In my experience, you'll do well by mastering a standard letter, with variations, and sending it to a large number of profiles.

Typical method:

Search within my criteria.

Open up various profiles of interest in separate tabs.

Read through each and contact any that immediately leap out (see the standard letters below).

Close profiles as you reply until you've completed your batch.

If, after a few passes, there's a profile that has you stuck, just send my *Amateur Hour* message or use the 'wink' function.*

Most sites have some kind of 'wink' or 'nudge' function. Sending an actual message is far, far superior but if you can't find anything to write about, it's better than nothing. Whether or not she responds to you will be based solely on the strength of your profile (if she even gets around to visiting it).

This uses an exam technique my high school math teacher taught us. We'd read through the paper and answer all of the easy and obvious questions first, leaving the rest of the time for questions that required more thought, in descending order of difficulty. So it is with your messages – hit the easiest, most interesting profiles first and then work your way down.

Standard Letters

My first weapon of choice:

Subject Line: *Bonus Points*

Message:

Hi X,

Your profile piqued my curiosity. It's refreshing to see someone with some [A] and [B]. Bonus points for [C]. Oh wait, you like [D]? Bonus points revoked immediately!

Sometimes, if a woman's profile is particularly bare, you can forgo this last line. It's better if you can include it, but it won't be possible on every occasion.

Good words for [A] and [B] include:

> Edge
>
> Individuality
>
> Passion

Humour

Openness

Adventurousness

Open-mindedness

Being well-traveled

Examples of [C] might include:

A sport or hobby

A cheesy band

A good band

A specific movie

*A physical compliment

Something in one of her pictures

A word on physical compliments. I don't favour these as a first choice, nor would I ever make them the main thrust of the message – it's too easy for the tone of such messages to be misread. I have had a degree of success throwing in one amidst the opening message when there's nothing in the profile worth complimenting. These are somewhat of a last resort.

As you can see, the things you give and take bonus points for don't matter – in fact, it's almost better if they're trivial. It's only a lighthearted way to establish humour themes, make your message stand out and give something for her to reply to.

For those women with very little text in their profile, try a variation of the following. It's something of a Hail Mary but it's worth a shot if you're playing the numbers game.

Subject Line: *Amateur Hour*

Message: *No 'about me' or 'interests' section... what is this, amateur hour?! ;) ***

If you like, you can soften this message with some kind of observation on whatever data her profile does contain. Say she has a picture of her on a boat:

P.S. Cool photo, I grew up around boats – are you a pirate?

Moving to the Phone

Having sent out your messages, you'll soon start getting profile views and replies. I will typically go to the phone after two or three on-site message exchanges. I keep these initial exchanges light, playful and fun and then send something like:

Message: *So listen, I'm not on here very often... drop me a text on [X], make me laugh ;)*

This is usually the ending line of a slightly larger message but it could be sent by itself. You could also, on a case by case basis, bring in an established humour theme to couch this request.

I personally don't go to instant messaging services. Frankly, I don't have the time and see it as something of a redundant step where much momentum can be lost. I'd much rather get to know a woman on a date than in a chat program. And, with some good on-site messaging and a solid profile, I've found that the vast majority of women who are interested will move to text quite easily. Remember, this is a numbers game, so don't worry too much about losing the occasional person.

If a woman counters my invitation to text with an invitation to chat on instant messenger, I'll typically say something like:

Message:

> *Hey,*
>
> *I don't use <insert name of messaging client>. Drop me a text and let's chat that way – I take my blackberry everywhere, it's practically attached to me :)*

From the Phone to the Date

Again, I'll move fairly quickly on this. Two, maybe three exchanges and then send the date text. I favour texting over calling, but at this point you're into standard follow up game so if you have a successful preference that differs from mine feel free to use it.

For more information on follow up game, check out Braddock and Mr. M's Phone and Text Game Ebook.

Conclusion

Online dating is a fantastic way to meet new women. When I first started experimenting online, I was amazed at how quickly and easily my schedule filled up with dates. With a strong profile, a good messaging system such as the one I've described, and a willingness to play the numbers, there's no reason why you can't soon enjoy similar success. Follow the information in this book, apply it to a steady stream of leads from your chosen dating site and your progression will be swift indeed.

Good luck and happy messaging!

Chapter 7: Cajun's Profile:
A Breakdown

by Keychain

Since I've now given you all this advice as to how to create your online dating profile, I thought it might be helpful if I included mine and went over it piece by piece with you. This way you can see how easy it is to incorporate all the advice I've given you without the profile looking like a cut and paste job. Let's begin!

Heading

Alright so the profile I'm going over is the one that I use on www.PlentyofFish.com which has a few features that other dating sites don't have. The first thing is the "headline" - it's basically the title of your profile. Let's see what I put:

Hordaleski The Barracuda : You need coolin, baby I ain't foolin.

Now, never mind the name and the fish, that's just there for this specific site as it makes you choose a fish to represent your personality I guess. The important part here is what comes after: "You need coolin, baby I ain't foolin." Recognize it? It's actually a lyric from a song by Led Zeppelin, one of my favourite bands. The importance here is that if they know the lyric it gives them a very easy way to message me. I often get messages saying "I LOVE Zeppelin! What's your favourite album?" which makes it very easy for me to keep the interaction going. Now, even if they don't recognize the lyric it's still a pretty cool thing to put as my headline since it has a cocky feel to it, so it's really win/win all things considered. Let's continue...

Basic Information

City: Vancouver British Columbia

Sign: Gemini

Height: 5' 8" (173 cm)

Age: 26 year old Man

Now these are all basic facts, so there's not much you can do here. I think I'm probably closer to 5'6

or 5'7 but I put 5'8 just because there are a lot of women out there who tend to look at height first when they're deciding if they want to read on, and I've found that 5'8 is usually their minimum requirement. Once they meet me I can use my personality to soften any blows that my false height may have caused; to be honest nobody has ever brought it up, and the truth is it doesn't really matter in the long run anyway. Moving on...

Personal Details

Smoker? No

Ethnicity: Mixed Race with Brown hair

Body Type: Athletic

Religion: Other Religion

So, there are a couple things here. Under ethnicity I put "mixed race with brown hair." Now I'm quite obviously Caucasian, and any woman would see that with my pictures. I mostly just put that so they would ask "What is your ethnic background?" which I've received as a first message quite a few times. To be truly honest I have a significant and traceable amount of native Mi'kmaq blood in me from a few generations back, so I'm not being completely facetious. Body type I put athletic, which is pretty much a lie, but if I flexed really hard and sucked in my chest I would definitely *look* athletic, which is good enough for me. Women lie about this all the time so I don't really have a problem with bending the truth on this one. If you are obese or terribly out of shape then I wouldn't lie too badly on this one. A rule of thumb is to ask yourself "Could I potentially look like someone with that body type with a shirt on?" If yes then go ahead and put it. By the time she sees you with your shirt off it won't really be an issue anymore, trust me.

For religion I put "Other Religion." I don't really follow any one religion; I suppose Buddhism would be the closest, but I wrote "other religion" to, again, bait them into messaging me asking which religion it is. I also didn't want to close myself out from either devout religious women, or devout non-religious women so it's a good neutral option. Now obviously if religion is important to you then you're going to want to specify that.

I am Seeking a: Woman (just for friends)

You know how I keep saying that your profile should communicate that you don't need online dating to meet women? That's why I listed "friends" as the women I'm seeking. I don't care if you really are looking for a wife, don't put that on here unless you want to meet psychos. Stick with "making friends."..for now.

Do you drink? Socially

Marital Status: Single

For these, there are a couple things you want to pay attention to. For drinking, I would say be honest, but if you drink quite a bit like I do. Then it's best to simply put "socially" instead of often. There are no women who find alcoholism attractive except other alcoholics, and believe me, you don't want to meet them. Marital status you should also be honest about. Hopefully you're single, but if you're not then there are better sites that use infidelity as their selling point (I.E. Ashleymadison.com) so you're better off using them unless you enjoy getting harassed.

Profession: Writer

Smarts: Bachelors degree

Do you want children? Undecided/Open

Profession is a big one. You obviously don't want to lie about what you do but you do want to make your job sound as appealing as possible. I put writer on mine, which isn't a lie since you're reading this book right now;

it's not the total truth but it does sound a hell of a lot better than "Pick-up artist" or even "dating coach." Try to find the most simple, appealing title to describe your job. If you own a network security company, even if it's a small start-up, put "business owner" instead of "Network security specialist." If you're a student taking engineering, put "engineering" and then in your profile mention that you're a student aspiring to start your own civil engineering firm or whatever you may be aspiring towards. Aspirations are nearly as good as real careers if women can sense you have a passion for them. If you have a boring job simply to pay the bills while you are working towards what you *really* want to do then put the career your working towards as your job and explain that in your profile. So if you work as a server but are trying to become an actor or musician then put actor or musician as your profession. It doesn't really matter if you haven't got paid for it yet, what matters is what you are aiming towards. If you had simply put "server" then a woman will assume you have no motivations and next you, even if you put "My real passion is music and I'm working on recording my own album... " later in your profile, she may never read it.

List your education if you have one, and for the wanting children option I'd just put undecided/open if the option exists. Even if you're dead set on not having kids you may turn women off and there's no way of knowing if you'll change your mind down the road. As well, if you definitely want kids I'd still put undecided/open just because you don't want the baby-crazy women going for you simply for your semen. Yes they exist, and the last thing you want is a woman screaming "Give me your baby batter!" right when it's too late to pull out. In fact I recommend always using condoms regardless - that's just a good rule.

Do you do drugs? No

Do you have children? No

Do you have a car? N/A

For drugs, even if you partake in the 420 I'd still put no. Women are going to assume the worst even if they're 420 friendly, and you don't want them thinking you're addicted to crack and other heavy stuff. With children I'd say be honest; I've talked to some people who claimed that they lied about it just to not scare women away right off the bat, and then slowly had them warm up to it after the first few dates. Maybe that's a route you'd like to take as well, but I've always found that honesty is the best policy for this. You don't want to get attached to a woman only to find that she hates kids and wants nothing to do with yours. If you're just planning on casually dating women and not getting involved with anyone, then yeah I guess you could lie about it. But they'll probably find out after a while anyways, so it's up to you.

Interests: Boats, Beaches, Bars, Beers, Beards, Bears, Blitzkriegs, Ballads, Barfights, and Pirates.

Ahhh interests! I already wrote a section on this and, as you can see, I've followed my own advice. It's pretty clear from the use of my alliteration and choice of interests that I'm not taking this too seriously. I've had women message me based solely on this, so it has been pretty successful. Now, you don't have to use musical devices in your interests for it to be interesting. If you have interesting... interests then by all means list them. If your profile lacks humour though, then this is a good place to start, as I mentioned earlier.

About Me Section

Alright, so that's the beginning of my profile, and at this point I'm already sounding like a pretty interesting person. A mixed-race athletic writer with an obscure religion and a sense of humour? *Who is this guy!?* Hopefully I've already hooked them, and if I have then they're going to be seeing the rest of my profile in a more attractive light, kind of like how funny movies always seem funnier if they have you laughing from the start. Now it's time for the meat of the profile though, and this is where I want to *really* hook them so that they feel compelled to message me. I'm going to let you read the whole thing through once so you can get a feel of how it should flow, and then I'm going to dissect it line by line and explain why I wrote what I did:

About Me:

> I'm 27 years old and I work as a writer/producer (and sometimes actor) for a media company which basically means I get to goof off and travel all over the world.

Who am I?

> I'm extremely artsy, I act, write, draw, paint, sing, play instruments, make films and take photographs.

> If that last line has you rolling your eyes, don't worry, I also drive fast, refuse to take shit from anyone, and am generally an asshole, but you know... the fun kind that's impossible to hate. If life were a movie I'd be a villain.

The villain you root for...

I'm the guy who is perfectly comfortable making the first move; whether it be a romantic kiss on the doorstep or throwing you up against a wall and making out with you HARD... in the rain.

I travel all over the world for work, so I'm out of town a lot... buuut I also take my friends along sometimes to keep me company. ;)

Most of my friends are artists (In a variety of mediums) so having an interest in the arts is pretty important.

I read a LOT, mostly history and philosophy.

I'm pretty mature for my age and am often labeled as "Wise beyond my years."

If we hang out there will never be an "awkward silence" don't worry, if you're nervous I will just tease you.

I have a fully black cat named Rod Stewart, he has bright green eyes and loves women... just like me.

I'm not looking for the trophy girlfriend, im much more

interested in personality. You don't have to be a model for me to respond, but if you are a model... please prove to me that you're ALL not bat sh*t crazy.

Hmmm what else...

I'm from New Brunswick, an avid outdoorsman and I miss the Atlantic. I think I'll just eventually buy my own Caribbean island and build a tree house. I recently moved to Vancouver and plan on living on my own sailboat and exploring the coast when I'm not writing.

I'm not taking this too seriously. I don't play mind games, nor do I placate low self-esteem. Until you impress me I will probably treat you like my bratty little sister.

P.S. If I send you a message that seems strange then I'm probably just bored and frigging with you. But also maybe im interested, it depends on how funny your reply is.

First Date:

How about I roll you up in a carpet and ship you to Greece? We could drive scooters through the countryside drinking wine and eating cheese, dress up in costumes, paint the sea and film the whole thing! I will make you my Mediterranean princess haha!

About Me Section Explained

Pretty good huh? Sounds like a pretty interesting guy doesn't it? There's a lot going on in what I wrote there, so, like I said, let's go through it line by line and I'll explain why I wrote it and what it means. OK, so the first line:

About Me:

I'm 26 years old and I work as a writer/producer (and sometimes actor) for a media company which basically means I get to goof off and travel all over the world.

I'm simply stating who I am in this line. They already have a basic idea from what was listed above, but this drives it home. I also act a bit humble with my profession in that even though it sounds important, I summarize it as "goofing off and travelling the world." This gives them a bit of my personality as well as reinforces the "I'm not trying to impress you" vibe that I want to communicate. I actually do own a media company where I write and produce commercials (as well as occasionally act in them) so for those of you screaming "LIAR."..I'm not.

Who am I?

I'm extremely artsy, I act, write, draw, paint, sing, play instruments, make films and take photographs.

So instead of just writing a paragraph about myself I opt for a list of qualities. This is more appealing to me because it makes it a lot easier for me to communicate my quality and character without over-writing. It's also a bit cocky since it's supposing that I know everything women are really looking for and I'll go ahead and list my "resume'" of sorts with an air of confidence. Think of your profile as a roller coaster ride; you want her to go through the ups and downs of the ride as she reads your profile. This means that if you're going to be cocky then just pepper it with cockiness as opposed to staying strong the whole way through. This first line is an example of that "peppering."

Also, with this first entry on the list I'm kind of setting myself up. I know that any woman who reads this line is probably going to be subconsciously rolling her eyes. It's a very cocky and braggy line (in fact it's too braggy) but since I have the benefit of hindsight, I know that she'll be won over by the end of my profile, and the roller coaster of emotions that gets elicited on the way there will, in the end, only make me more appealing. Also, it's all true.

> *If that last line has you rolling your eyes, don't worry, I also drive fast, refuse to take shit from anyone, and am generally an asshole, but you know... the fun kind that's impossible to hate. If life were a movie I'd be a villain. The villain you root for...*

So with this next line I'm showing a little bit of self-reflexive social intelligence. As I said earlier, I knew she would be rolling her eyes at that last line, so this line justifies the cockiness of it and then redeems me by showing that I'm also savvy to the imperfection of it. This line also plays into the "bad boy" image quite strongly; what woman doesn't love a charming villain? Notice the language I use to describe my quality? I describe my confidence as a fault, and then make no apologies about it. I talked about this earlier and it's the easiest way to brag about yourself; present your strengths as faults and then make no apologies about them.

> *I'm the guy who is perfectly comfortable making the first*
> *move; whether it be a romantic kiss on the doorstep or*
> *throwing you up against a wall and making out with you*
> *HARD... in the rain.*

This line hits on what I talked about earlier in the profile section: letting her know I have balls and won't make things awkward when it comes to romance. I also, again, show social intelligence by saying I realize that there are situations that call for romance and situations that call for strong sexually charged advances and that I'm experienced and confident enough to handle both. This is a strong line and I frequently get women messaging me stating that it was this line that got them turned on enough to message me. Again, pay attention to the strong visually descriptive language. Throwing her up against a wall and making out with her? Normally I'd say that's too cheesy of a line, but the fact that I overdo it by adding ."..in the rain" implies that I'm not taking the description seriously. I'm saying exactly what she wants to hear not necessarily because I want her to believe I possess these qualities, but because I want her to know that *I know exactly what she wants to hear and will make fun of her for it!* It's this self-reflexive voice that truly communicates sexual experience and intelligence.

> *I travel all over the world for work, so I'm out of town a lot...*
> *buuut I also take my friends along sometimes to keep me*
> *company. ;)*

When a woman is attracted to a man, she is naturally going to start fantasizing what it would be like to be a part of his life. This line indicates that I must have a pretty exciting life, as I'm constantly travelling. Normally this could have a tendency to turn women off, since it simply means I'm away a lot, but I change the visual a bit by forcing her to think about travelling to exotic locales *with* me, and that, maybe, I'd foot the bill, which is going to make her assume I have money to do so. So far it has never happened...

Most of my friends are artists (In a variety of mediums) so having an interest in the arts is pretty important.

So, this line communicates a couple things. Firstly it says I have a lot of cool friends, whom I'll probably introduce her to, which again adds fuel to the fantasy of her becoming a part of my life. She's naturally going to start imagining herself hanging out with a bunch of cool filmmakers, painters and musicians. It also states that I have standards, that I'm looking for something specific and that she's going to have to prove herself to meet my minimum requirements.

I read a LOT, mostly history and philosophy.

With this one I'm just communicating that I'm intelligent. It's also a good hook though; if there are any women who also have an interest in history or philosophy there's a good chance that they may use that as an opportunity to message me. I actually do read quite a bit about history and philosophy so if she did message me I could have a discourse about it with her and use it as an opportunity to push the interaction forward. For example, "You're cute AND intelligent, I like that, but playing email tag on an internet dating site is pretty lame, you should give me your number and I'll give you a call later and we can converse like normal people. There's this incredible book I need to talk to you about!"

I'm pretty mature for my age and am often labelled as "Wise beyond my years."

I was actually interested in dating older women for a while, so I put this line up so they knew that I wasn't an immature goof. I suppose maturity could be considered sexy, but I only put this down because I'm young. If you're over thirty then I wouldn't bother with this one.

If we hang out there will never be an "awkward silence" don't worry, if you're nervous I will just tease you.

I mentioned this line earlier when I talked about your "about me" section. Essentially I'm quelling any fears she may have about an awkward first date. As I said, this not only puts her mind at ease for the date, but it also shows that I'm socially intelligent enough to know that it probably happens quite a bit, and that I'm not one of those guys.

I have a fully black cat named Rod Stewart, he has bright green eyes and loves women... just like me.

This is a great "real" line. It's dropping the act a bit and revealing some true information about me, and it also communicates a bit of character too. Who names their cat Rod Stewart? I do, mostly because I wanted to give my cat a dumb name because he bites a lot and is an asshole. Women have messaged me saying that it's hilarious I named my cat after Rod, which is an easy hook, but I wouldn't recommend going out and getting a pet just so you can name it something stupid to make your profile funnier.

The second part *"and loves women, just like me"* is simply implying that I'm aware of my scandalous character traits and admire them enough to explicitly state them. Being a lover of women suggests that I must have the experience to back that up, so it's just a little wordplay to subtly get that idea into their head.

> *I'm not looking for the trophy girlfriend, I'm much more interested in personality. You don't have to be a model for me to respond, but if you are a model... please prove to me that you're ALL not bat shit crazy.*

This is probably my favourite line in the whole profile. I wanted to imply that I have dated beautiful women, but how do you do that without coming across as braggy, especially if you're stating that they were models? That's a tough nut to crack, but this line does it perfectly. The first part is essentially saying "If you've read this far and think that you're not up to par for my standards, that's OK, because I'm really interested in personality." That was actually a concern of mine when I created the profile: that women would feel I was *too* good to be true, or that they weren't good enough to message me. A little presumptuous maybe, but I found my inbox twice as busy after I added this line in.

The second part basically says "I've dated numerous models and it's really annoying because they're all fucking crazy and just add unnecessary drama. So I'm done with them, and now I want someone beautiful AND cool." Obviously a guy who dates models on a regular basis is perceived as a high value man. The way to communicate this "high value" without appearing overly braggy is to disguise it as "low value." So in this case I'm saying, "yes I've dated models, but it really SUCKED." It's still tremendously cocky, but coupled with the rest of my profile, it doesn't stick out as much as it should. So if you are going to use a line like this make sure that you have an overall "cocky" attitude with your profile otherwise this one will stick out like a sore thumb and women will simply roll their eyes.

The other interesting thing that this line communicates is that not only have I dated models, but I was the one who, presumably, ended things. Not only that, but I've dated enough of them to establish a jaded stereotype about their character. I then go on to say that models shouldn't feel discriminated against as long as they can prove to me that they're normal and cool... wait a second... did I just state that MODELS are going to have to prove to ME that they're cool if they want a chance? That's a pretty fucking pimp belief to establish; I'm setting myself up as a prize before the first message is even sent!

So at this point in the profile they're probably again asking themselves the question: "Who the fuck is this guy? This successful writer who travels all over the world, hangs out with filmmakers and musicians, dates models and has a cat named Rod Stewart!?" Well, the thing is, at this point I have to start being a little more real. Constructing a profile is a lot like building a house of cards: you want to get as high as you can but one wrong move and the whole thing collapses. Right now I'm coming across as a pretty damn interesting guy, but I lack depth to my character; I'm a caricature of my true self. I've added in plenty of braggy bits, so now it's time to get real!

Hmmm what else...

> *I'm from New Brunswick, an avid outdoorsman and I miss the Atlantic. I think I'll just eventually buy my own Caribbean island and build a tree house. I recently moved to Vancouver and plan on living on my own sailboat and exploring the coast when I'm not writing.*

Alright, so this says a few things about me: Where I'm from, what I'm like, and some of my goals. I actually changed this when I moved from Toronto to Vancouver to reflect the differences. People in Vancouver tend to love the outdoors more and the fact that I'm from N.B. And miss the Atlantic is different enough to west coasters that they may feel inclined to ask about it. Being from the east coast is actually a big part of my identity as well, similar to how a New Yorker living in L.A. would identify strongly with other New Yorkers, so anyone living in Vancouver who is also from the east coast is probably going to want to message me based on that alone. I also give a bit of a glimpse into my life when I talk about living on a sailboat and exploring when I'm not writing. This again makes me seem more three dimensional as a person.

> *I'm not taking this too seriously. I don't play mind games, nor do I placate low self-esteem. Until you impress me I will probably treat you like my bratty little sister.*

Alright, so I openly state that I'm not taking the site seriously, if they haven't already guessed that. I also say a bit of a cocky line when I tell them I'll treat them like my bratty sister until they impress me. This again sets me up as a challenge, and any self confident woman will read that and think "This guy sounds like someone who has a lot of options." That is exactly what I want to communicate at this point. Women don't want the guy who walks on eggshells, they want the guy who doesn't give a fuck and is willing to lose her.

> *P.S. If I send you a message that seems strange then I'm probably just bored and frigging with you. But also maybe I'm interested, it depends on how funny your reply is.*

I actually just put this in recently. If you haven't already noticed from reading some of my message templates, I tend to send some pretty bizarre messages. I noticed that a lot of the time these women were visiting my profile so I put up that little disclaimer at the end so they would know I was just playing with them and not actually crazy. It also sets up a challenge to send me something funny back as well as implying that I have standards when it comes to how clever they are.

> *First Date*
>
> *How about I roll you up in a carpet and ship you to Greece? We could drive scooters through the countryside drinking wine and eating cheese, dress up in costumes, paint the sea and film the whole thing! I will make you my Mediterranean princess haha!*

This is simply a future adventure projection, which I talked about earlier. These are great for baiting women into messaging you. With this one I've received messages as simple as "I was just in Greece! I love it there!" or "Oh my god I am a cheese connoisseur and I will totally take you up on that!"

Chapter 7: The Question Game

Here it is! Finally, what you've all been waiting for... MY SUPER SECRET ROUTINE! That's right, for the first time ever I'm finally making my most coveted routine available to the masses. Why is this such a big deal? Well, if you've heard about this routine then you already know, but for those who haven't let's go over some of the specifics:

I'm about to give you the best routine you will ever use for what we call the comfort phase of getting to know someone, or the stage in which you build trust by finding commonalities, sharing personal stories, and learning intimate details about each other.

I, as well as all my friends and students who have learned this routine, still continue to use it on nearly every date we go on.

If you get to the end of the routine there's about an 80% chance of things turning sexual (more on that later).

The routine can take up the entire date. That's right, it's the only tool you need (besides your penis) to ace every date you go on from now on.

The only routine I know of that single-handedly breaks downs barriers and opens up sexual threads of conversation in a way that women find extremely entertaining and impossibly hard to resist.

Introduction

So how did this routine come about?

Well, the reason I felt that this routine would be a great addition to this book specifically is because its culmination was very well connected to my research into online dating. I mentioned at the beginning of the book that I had turned to online dating initially because I had wanted to set up as many dates as possible as a way to work on my ability to become an amazing first date. Well, very early on I realized that if I was going to be critical of my dating abilities I would need to create a blueprint for the date which I could add to and tweak until I broke it down to the core qualities that make a great first date.

To find the structure or frame to base the date around I actually ended up turning to my peers at Love Systems. The "question game" had already been around for quite some time, and was well known as a great comfort routine. I had read posts by some of the major players at Love Systems at the time and the question game frequently came up as a great routine to use in the comfort phase or on a date. The basic premise was that you take turns asking each other questions and it's your job to make the questions become more and more sexual. I thought that this was a great frame that I could use for all my dates and that my main hurdle was going to be perfecting the questions themselves.

Since I couldn't find very many good examples online as to which questions to ask, I decided to simply jump head first into the whole process and go on as many dates as it took for me to figure out the best questions, and ultimately find out what the core qualities that make a great first date are... So that's exactly what I did.

For several months I played the question game on every single date I went on. This is no small feat either, considering that I had become so proficient with online dating that I was now lining up about four dates a week (much to my roommate's disdain). I played around with a number of different questions, exploring the extremes of both personal and sexual topics (or both simultaneously) and managed to mess up quite a few dates by either going too far in one direction or the other. In the end though, which surmounted to quite a few dozen dates, I had figured out through trial and error the exact core qualities that women look for on a first date, and how to elicit these qualities simply by the questions that I ask. More importantly, I had figured out the exact questions to ask, the order to ask them in, the exact timing and wording as well as the body language to assume in order to turn the date sexual about eighty percent of the time.

Think about that for a second... using one routine I had managed to turn eighty percent of my first dates sexual. That's HUGE! There's no other routine that I know of that can even come close to those odds, but why eighty percent? Why not one hundred percent!? Well, something that I ended up realizing is that even though most women will state that they do not sleep with men on the first date, only about twenty percent of them will outright refuse the possibility of things going sexual even if they really want to. The reasons for this are numerous and not really worth getting into unless you wanted me to devote a whole chapter to female psychology. The curious thing, however, is that of those twenty percent who may have denied my advances on the first date, nearly all of them were ready and willing to turn things sexual on the second date. So if were looking at this in terms of a timeline, this routine pretty much has a 100% success rate over time if you can manage the few hurdles that may spring up.

OK, so enough of the hype, let's get to the routine already! Well before I get to the routine itself I need to give you a few tips to make sure that the game works as well as it should. This is a game where you can shoot yourself in the foot quite easily by not thinking ahead and I want to make sure you guys are in the best possible position no matter what. So let's go over a few ground rules:

Basics of the Question Game

First of all, only use this routine when you are ALONE with your woman. Do not play this game in front of her friends! That is a surefire way to ruin the game and possibly get blown out. Be patient, and wait until you can play the game with her when her friends can't hear what you're doing. Sometimes this means waiting until you can grab a seat with her, sometimes it means waiting until her back is to her friends at the bar, depending on how ballsy you are.

There are two versions of this game: the date version and the bar version. The only difference is that with the date version you want to ask several "fluff" questions before you get into the questions that I give you. "Fluff" questions are simple "getting to know you" type questions that introduce your date to the game without raising any questions as to why you're doing so. Example questions would be things like "What's the most beautiful place you've ever visited?" or "What's your all time favourite song and why?" You want fluff questions that are both positive and a little personal, but nothing sexual at this point. The bar version of the game doesn't really require "fluff" questions because since this game is played in comfort, you've most likely already been talking to her and qualifying for the past ten or so minutes, so it's fine to start sexual with the first question that I give you for the game.

If on a date, be sure to get a table that is a little secluded, like a booth in the corner. You want some privacy so your date doesn't start to feel self-conscious or embarrassed if other people can hear what you're talking about.

If you're in the bar and you have a friend winging you, do NOT play the game in tandem. As soon as they go to the washroom (and they will if they're both playing the game and liking you guys) they will talk about the questions and quickly find out that everything was scripted. Not only will this ruin the interaction but you will both look seriously creepy in the process. This happened to me once and it was NOT fun trying to explain to the women why we had asked the exact same questions. Either keep it to yourself or plan ahead with your buddy to avoid this.

Alright, so let's get to the game. Before I begin I want to stress that you pay VERY close attention to the way I write the questions down. A lot of information is conveyed in the way you say these questions and since I'm not standing in front of you right now demonstrating the exact way to enunciate these words to get your subtext correct, you're going to have to pay close attention to the way I write them down to get the correct meaning. I will give thorough explanations for the important questions, but for the rest pay extra attention to things like commas and ellipses; they carry more weight than you think.

To start the game you're going to say the following:

> *"Hmm, we don't know each other very well, so... we should play a game to get to know each other."*

Watch how she reacts. If she seems apprehensive or sceptical, you may need extra fluff questions. Act as if you're thinking of a good game to play then say:

> *"Have you ever played the question game?"*

There's about a 95% chance that she will say no to this, however some women will claim that they have. That's fine, I actually remember playing the game when I was a kid at parties, so it's not like you're getting caught using an opener you heard on TV or anything. Keep going regardless.

> *"Yeah, it's simple, we're just going to take turns asking each other questions... there are rules though."*

Before you tell her the rules you want to act like you're thinking about what the rules should be. Don't dwell too long on this, otherwise it will come across forced and you'll end up looking fake. Just pause for a second and then continue, as if you're making the rules up as you go along.

"Rule number one:

You can't ask the same question twice.

So if I ask you a question, you can't ask me the same question back."

She'll probably ask you what happens when you break a rule, so just tell her you'll figure that out when it happens. But it will NOT BE GOOD. Or just jokingly tell her that if she breaks a rule she loses the game and you will think less of her. It doesn't really matter anyways, since she will want to keep playing the game as soon as she gets a few questions in.

"Rule number two:

If you refuse to answer a question, you lose the game."

This is the most important rule because it gives you an excuse to ask very personal and sexual questions with the out of "I'm just trying to win the game." The importance of this rule comes up in question three, so be sure to emphasize this one.

"Rule number three:

You're allowed one follow up question, per question."

She'll probably ask about his one, so just tell her that it essentially means you get two questions per turn but it's optional. I usually use the example of "If you asked me what my favourite car was, and I answered "Ferrari" you could follow up with something like "What colour would it be?" The other good thing about using that question as an example is that it lets her believe that the game is going to be based around very general getting to know you type questions.

> *"Rule number four:*
> *I go first."*

Pretty self-explanatory. Say it jokingly, as if you already thought of the perfect first question.

Running the Routine

Alright! So now that the rules are out of the way, now come the questions! Remember, if you're on a date you don't want to jump right into the first question, you'll want to do some fluff ones first as I explained earlier, so keep that in mind.

> *Question #1*
> *"How many guys have you been with... romantically?"*

Obviously you want her to take this one as "How many guys have you slept with?" without actually saying that. The ellipses here are very important, so you need her to jump to her own conclusions about the sexuality of this question. If you don't and she thinks you're simply finding a clever way to ask how many guys she's fucked you may find some confrontation or resistance with this one, so try to make it a little ambiguous. Women will usually respond one of two ways to this question; they'll either say "What, do you mean sex?" in which you will say "Sure" as if that's not what you meant, but that's just as good. Or she will say "What do you mean by romantic?" in which case you will say "What do you think I mean!?"

If she presses further or takes the question in a negative way, then you'll need to use a fail-safe response. So let's say she says "No, really what do you mean by romantic?" or "This question is a little personal..." then just use the follow-up response of "Huh? How many romantic relationships have you been in?" as if that's what you meant all along. This is obviously a completely different question so only use that re-wording if you absolutely have to. The reason we want them to answer the question as "how many guys have you slept with?" is because, as guys, WE DO NOT WANT TO BE ASKED THAT QUESTION. That's why it's the first question, because for us there may not be a good answer to that. If our number is low: it's bad, if it's high: it's bad, if it's somewhere in the middle... it could be bad. There's no way of knowing. Although if you're absolutely fucked and you have to reword the question with the fail-safe and she asks it for her next question, then obviously telling the truth would be the best answer, but if you're unwilling to do that, here's a handy chart you can use:

Aged:
18-25: 10-15 women.
25-30: 15-20 women.
30-40: 25+ women.

Those are pretty good numbers for the ages, and you won't look like a slut or a slouch. Although I always advise telling the truth I do understand that in some cases that can ruin things.

Now remember that no matter what number she gives you for her answer: DO NOT BE JUDGEMENTAL. That means no responses like "Wow!" or "That's quite a bit!" or even "That's it?" You don't know how she may feel about her number or if she's even telling the truth, so try not to shoot yourself in the foot by being judgemental when there's a good chance that she may be self-conscious about her answer.

Question 1: Follow up
"When was the last one?"

So hopefully she took the first question the correct way and now your follow up is essentially "when was the last time you had sex?" this is good for a couple of reasons. Firstly she is going to feel like you're qualifying her with the question, which is great, but more importantly she's going to have to remember when the last time she had sex was. In order to remember that she's going to have to visualize it. Remember what I said about how women have very visual minds? In the first question you already have her qualifying herself to you as well as visualizing having sex. Not bad, but let's continue.

Question #2
"What was your longest relationship?"

Question 2: Follow up
"When did it end?"

This is a good question to ask simply because if you're actually interested in dating the woman, this can give some valuable information. For instance, if her longest relationship was ten years, and it ended two weeks ago, you're probably not going to be getting into a serious relationship with her anytime soon. Likewise, if her longest relationship was two weeks, again, not much long term potential here, although a one night stand could be an obvious option. This question is also quite a bit softer than the first question, so it helps move the game forward without her thinking that you're going to have a bunch of sexual questions firing one after another. This entire game takes a two steps forward-one step back approach, and this is the step back from the first one. If she had any doubts as to the intention of the game from the first question, this one will usually quell them since it's very safe, and a somewhat interesting question. It also encourages her to ask more relationship or sexually themed questions which is exactly what you want at this early point in the game.

Alright, so question number three...

This is where things get a little interesting. Before you even ask the third question you have to pre-emptively give her the reason why you're asking it. So, you want to say:

> *"Alright, if I want to win this game I have to start asking the tough questions. Hmm, what's a question I don't think you would answer... oh, I know!"*

Try not to make this sound too scripted; this is probably the most important question in the game.

Question #3

"When was the last time... you masturbated?"

It's extremely important that you ask this question as if you just won the game. Say it as if you just checkmated her, as if you DARE her to answer the question. This is going to bait her into answering it even if she doesn't necessarily think it's something you should be told. The subtext here isn't "I want to know when you last masturbated." It's "I bet you don't have the balls to answer this question." So ask the question with that intention.

Now, women are going to respond to this question in one of three different ways:

About 50% of women will answer straight up without batting an eye. This has more to do with how women look at masturbation. As men we look at masturbation as something shameful and somewhat embarrassing, but most women tend to view their masturbation as an extension of their sexuality so it's nothing really worth hiding. Don't act surprised when they answer so nonchalantly, in fact act as if she just got bonus points with you for being cool about it. Lean back, smirk approvingly and move on to the follow up question.

About 45% of women will give you hell for asking the question, but will still answer it in the end. They'll say things like "Oh my god I can't believe you asked me that!?" or "That's so personal!" They're not necessarily saying these because they're embarrassed about answering the question itself. What they're really embarrassed about is how you would think of them if they answered up front without giving you shit first. Some women are upfront and honest about their sexuality, while some hide it behind the morality that was instilled into them from a young age. Most, however, will give in to the thrill of an openly sexual discourse with an attractive stranger if given the chance to in a discreet way. That's exactly what this game is for and is exactly why this question is the most important in the game; it's the sexual turning point.

About 5% of women will outright refuse to answer the question. It's actually probably lower than 5% because it has only happened to me twice in the 100 or so times I've played this game, but it does come up. Actually the last time it happened, I was playing it with an extremely conservative and religious woman, so I should have seen it coming. Oh well, sometimes it's hard to get people to do things that will *most likely result in them going to hell*. So what now though? Let's say she says "No, I'm not answering that." Well, your first step is to let her know that she'll lose the game if she refuses to answer the question, so say "Really? (as if you can't believe she would refuse to answer such an easy question) Well you realize that you'll lose the game if you don't answer?" If she still won't budge then don't worry, I got you covered, say:

"Alright, well there's actually something I didn't tell you about before, and that is that there's actually a fifth rule to the game that allows you one "turn-around" per game. A

> *turn-around let you take a question that you were asked and*
> *flip it onto the person who asked, so they have to answer it.*
> *But you can only use it once in the game; are you sure you*
> *want to use it now?"*

She'll most likely know that you're basically bullshitting your way into keeping the game going, but that's OK because it gives her an easy out to avoid the question anyways. She should respond with "OK" or "sure."

So now you have to answer when the last time you masturbated was. Tease her a bit first for not answering the question when it was her turn, so say things like "Hmm, last time I masturbated? Currently, that's why my hand has been in my pocket the last 7 minutes (say 7 mins as if it's an impressive amount of time)" or "I masturbated when I went to the washroom earlier... " This will relieve the tension of her not answering the question when it was her turn as well as tease her a bit for taking it so seriously. Eventually though give her the correct answer in a way that communicates that you have no problem giving up that information and then move on with the game.

Question 3: Follow up
"Where was it?"

I mentioned before that women have extremely visual minds. So when you ask a question like this, it forces the woman to actually remember where she was when she was turned on enough to masturbate, and when she remembers she actually visualizes, and thus re-lives the act of masturbation. Again, you're putting her into a position here where she can not only be comfortable vocalizing her sexuality but also, to a certain extent, be comfortable physically with her sexual desires. This is extremely powerful and is something that women really only open up about when they're with their best friends.

Alright so it's her turn again. She's probably going to want revenge on you for asking the masturbation question so be prepared to answer some tough questions. Some examples I've heard:

Have you ever been in love?

Have you ever cheated?

How big is your dick?

How long can you last?

You can always lie, but for some, like how big your dick is, you may have to put your money where your mouth is later on (or her mouth if you're lucky). So don't shoot yourself in the foot if you can help it.

At this point, if she doesn't ask you a question that's even remotely sexual, you'll need to address that. So, for instance, let's say she asks "What's your favourite book?" You will need to reply with something akin to "Pfff, you're never going to win the game asking questions like that... try again." If she persists, and says "No, really what's your favourite book?" simply roll your eyes as if she doesn't understand the game and then answer. Try not to give her any pleasure with your answer, don't be pouty or anything, but just answer the question and then get excited that it's your turn again and you can ask a "good" question to turn the game back on track.

Question #4

"Where is the craziest place you've ever had sex?"

If you haven't already noticed, the questions tend to take dips in their provocativeness. It's the old two steps forward, one step back rule, and it works well to smoothly escalate the conversation forward into more sexually explicit topics without raising any alarms as to your reasoning or intentions. This question, you may notice, is a tad less risky than the previous and would be considered a step back. This is to quell any notion within the woman's mind that the game may veer into more perverse territory if your questions are left unchecked. It's somewhat safe, and it keeps the game moving forward.

There's a certain element of bravado established with this question as well in that it presupposes that she has sex in interesting places, which implies that YOU often have sex in interesting places and that you simply assume everyone else does as well (hence your asking). This not only makes you come across as someone with sexual prowess, but it also puts her in a position where she has to qualify to you. This is why you'll often receive responses of "Ahh, hmm I haven't done anything REALLY good but... " or "Well, this isn't that crazy but... " before she answers. All this means is that she is assuming that she can't match up to your supposed sexual experiences and is trying to qualify herself to you.

The other obvious benefit to this question is the fact that she's going to have to remember having sex in a situation that was a little scandalous. This not only helps put her in a sexual state, but it also builds some trust and comfort with you since she is revealing something that she probably has only told her good friends.

Question 4: Follow up
"You gotta tell me that story"

This question is to simply have her expand on her answer to the initial question. If her answer is something quite interesting like "In an oven" then you're most likely going to want to know how it happened anyway. It lets her relive the experience again, experiencing the same emotions, except with you this time. It also builds more trust and comfort for the same reasons as mentioned above: it's probably something she's only told to those very close to her.

Feel free to have conversations between the questions as well if it comes naturally. One of the reasons this game works so well for dates is because it promotes a natural flow of conversation. If there's ever an awkward silence or pause, you can always go back to the game by saying "Alright, so whose turn is it?" It makes the game feel much more organic and natural as opposed to something more planned and objective driven. It also makes it easier to escalate the questions if she's had time to get to know you in between them.

Question #5

"What's your favourite position?"

Obviously, she's going to know what you mean by "position." The purpose of this question isn't necessarily to find out what her favourite sexual position is (although that will be very helpful for later), the purpose of asking this question is so that you can insinuate that you will be having sex with her in the immediate future. This is done by how you respond to her answer. Whatever position she answers with, you're going to respond the exact same way, even if it's the most messed up or disgusting position you've ever heard. So:

Cajun: What's your favourite position?

Jasmine: Hmm probably doggy style.

Cajun: Really? Nice, me and you are going to get along.

Notice the bold italic print? You're going to respond with that no matter what she says, and you want to say it like you just realized that she has the exact same favourite position as you. By saying that you're going to get along you're obviously implying that you're going to have sex. You're not asking, or hoping that you will, you're explicitly saying that you're going to, and not only that, but it's also going to be great sex. Double win! This also frames the interaction as "both of us can't wait to have sex with each other because were so compatible." Which, as long as she's having fun with the game, she will be accepting of.

Often you will have women that may not know the name of, or have a hard time explaining their favourite position. This is fine, and I usually tease them a bit for not knowing how to explain it, which if they're a little embarrassed about makes it even better. Ask her to show you with her hands but get involved using your hands too. So make a little man out of your fingers and say "OK so am I laying down? Standing up?" and then get her to position hers where she would be. Then react with statements like "Oh yes, that would work, I like it!" or "Oh yeah, this looks fun!" The point here is to get her comfortable doing something that is a reflection of what might happen later, and obviously the more comfortable the better.

This is usually the point in the game when you're going to start noticing a difference in how she's acting. She will be leaning in more, making excuses to touch you, getting excited about the next question. Try to keep cool, maintain a sly smile and reward her answers with flirty smiles and touching when you can. Be aware of your own body language as well. If you're on a date and sitting at a table and she's not leaning in then you should maintain a laid back attitude as well. When she does come close, lean in and touch her hand in a platonic kind of way. A small touch can go a long way at this point, especially since the sexual tension is starting to mount considerably. Sometimes I may take her hand and do a cold read just so I have an excuse to touch her and escalate things physically, but it's not required. Feel things out for yourself given the logistics.

Now, a lot of people usually ask "What if she asks one of your questions before you do?" In practice, this doesn't usually happen, but when it does it's usually this question. To combat this I'm giving you two separate follow up questions so that you can use the unused one as your go-to question if she happens to ask the favourite position question before you do.

Question 5: Follow ups
"What's one thing you've always wanted to try sexually, but haven't?"

or

"What's your secret, or not so secret fetish?"

These questions are fairly similar, but different enough that even if you ended up asking both, you would most likely get different answers. Both do however, deal with subjects that women might not be very forthcoming with, whether it be with you, or possibly even themselves. This, again, is good since it promotes the conversational thread of open sexual honesty that this game has been based around. Be extra careful with these questions and remember to always reward her answers by not putting forth even a hint of judgement. She may have a hard time answering them, and if you react with something like "Hmm that's kind of weird" or "seriously?" it may very well ruin the entire game and her trust in you. Whatever weird kinky stuff she's into, just act as if you're also into weird stuff and you're glad that you could both talk about it without getting embarrassed or judgemental with each other. This is another one of those questions which can push you forward into the "OK I really want to fuck this guy" category, so it's extra important to be careful with it.

Question #6

"On a scale of 1-10, how would you rate yourself in the sack?"

For my non-North American readers, "in the sack" simply refers to "in bed." So essentially this question is asking "Are you a good fuck?" As a general rule, you're going to respond the same no matter what she answers, which I'll explain to you in a second. But just so you're aware, here's what the different numbers mean:

If she answers:

> 1-4 -She's probably fucking with you or joking. Funny women usually respond with this.
>
> 5-7 -She's probably being honest. Self-confident women usually respond with this.
>
> 8-10 (or higher) -She's qualifying herself to you, and in the

case that it's higher than 10, wants you to know that she wants to fuck you.

Now, like I said, no matter what number she gives you you're going to respond exactly the same, which is:

"Nice, I'm a ___"

That blank there is whatever her number is plus one. So if she says "I'm a 3." you would say "Nice! I'm a 4!" or likewise, if she said "I'm definitely a 10" you would say "Nice, I'm an 11." See how that works? Even if she tries to be funny or cocky, your reaction trumps it. It's one of the few times in the game where there's a one size fits all response available, so take advantage of it.

This is also really the first question in the game that's explicitly about you two having sex, without any word play or innuendo involved. It's also a very good question to determine how well the game has worked on her. If you've gotten this far, don't worry, there's definitely attraction, but how difficult it may be to escalate things from this point can be communicated by how she answers this. If she answers high, with an almost braggy tone, then there's a good chance she's been thinking about fucking you and has already made the decision. If she answers lower, she may be being honest and doesn't want to give you false expectations about her ability, this could be a sign of self-confidence or low self-esteem, ironically. Women who answer very low are probably seeing the question for what it is and teasing you for asking it. This is still good but it means that she may give you some resistance down the road as well, and isn't necessarily ready to totally give in to your charms just yet.

Whatever the case, the follow up tends to address it.

> *Question #6: Follow up*
> *"What about oral?"*

I'm just going to assume that everyone loves blow jobs, otherwise you may be out of luck for this question. Now, much like the previous question, the obvious context here is "How good at blow jobs are you?" but your subtext should be "How well will you suck MY dick?" See the difference? This is actually the question that when a client of mine got to it in the game at a bar in Vancouver, the woman simply took his hand, whispered "Let me show you" and brought him into the washroom. This is a powerful question, and is the most explicitly sexual of all of them given the context of when it's said in the game. She's already attracted to you, and by making her answer how well she would suck your dick, you escalate things to a place where the only way to go further is to actually start having sex (or getting a BJ). Very few women would have this conversation with a man they didn't plan on having sex with.

Don't worry about responding with the "Nice, I'm a... " for this one. In fact you're going to purposely remain silent on your ability. Respond with something like "Interesting... " and smile confidently while glancing down at her lips as if you know what's going to happen in the immediate future. She may ask "What about you?" Just say "Ah, can't ask the same question, remember?" and then add "You'll just have to wait and find out." followed by a shit-eating grin.

Now, at this point the sexual tension should be just about through the roof. You can't really go any further without making a move to release some of the tension, so that's exactly what we're going to do. Once it's your turn again you're going to go for the final question of the game. If you're sitting across from each other at a table or a booth then you're going to need to close that gap. Say the following:

"Alright, my next question is really dirty and I don't want anyone to hear. So I'm gonna come over here..."

Simply slide your chair over or sit next to her in the booth and then whisper in her ear:

Question #7
"Are you... a good kisser?"

After you ask this, slowly back away from her face, but stay close, and look down at her lips and smile. If she doesn't answer just go in for the kiss. If she does answer, it doesn't really matter what she says, she'll still kiss you at this point. The only instance when she wouldn't is if there are a lot of people around and she doesn't want them to see. Just pay attention to her body language, it should be fairly easy to read. Don't do any crazy make-outs or ram your tongue down her throat. Make it sexy and romantic at the same time, and remember: she's been thinking about doing this for a good while now, so don't disappoint. End the kiss first, and then slowly back your face away and smile.

Something that I usually do at this point is to call attention to the impact of the kiss. It was the first kiss, and most likely has turned her on quite a bit, so to add to the impact of that I'll say something like:

> *"Oh man, you know what's weird? You know when you kiss someone for the first time there's always those first few seconds when you're trying to figure out how each other kisses? Well, we seem to kiss like we've kissed many times before. That's cool, I like that."*

And that's the game! At this point you're obviously going to want to get alone with her. You can usually just say something like "Let's get out of here." or "Let's go have some wine back at my place." and they'll usually be fine with that. When you leave the bar, as soon as you get somewhere a bit private, whether that be in the alley or in your car, you want to go for another kiss. Much like the first kiss, this is going to be to release some of that sexual tension and amp up the vibe for what's about to happen when you get back to your place. I'm calling it a kiss and not a make-out because you don't want to release too much sexual tension at this point; just enough to entice her to want more, so I wouldn't throw my tongue down or feel her up or anything, wait until you're back at your place for the heavy stuff. Once back at your place, the wine should be an afterthought. Simply take her to your room or the couch and get to business. You shouldn't have much resistance at this point.

Chapter 9: Message Logs

These are some conversational threads I have had through dating sites to give you an idea of the type of teasing involved and the speed at which you can turn a friendly conversation into something much more flirty.

Message Log 1 Carla

#1 – Carla messages me

[Carla]: My interest in beards is not a rhetorical stylistic device. Is yours genuine?

(Remember I used alliteration to describe my interests.)

[Cajun]: Definitely, I have a beard right now, in fact I only have two different styles; Beard, and beard construction. I'm pretty much an old man though, I drink scotch, I like boats, I like butterscotch. I am also addicted to guacamole.

(Her profile mentioned how she can make a mean guacamole.)

[Carla]: That sounds delightful. Beards are undoubtedly a gift from the heavens.

My brother recently married a Mexican girl simply so that we could steal her family's top secret guacamole recipe. Actually, that's not at all why but I have the recipe now and I make guacamole at least once a week. I win.

Have you ever considered wearing a monocle?

[Cajun]: I was thinking of wearing a monocle with the eyepatch yeah. I think they would go well. Hmm you have a secret guac recipe huh? This does not bode well if you had planned on me not bugging you to make me some everytime I see you. Because I will... and if you don't have any I'll be like "That's ok I was just joking" but secretly I wasn't and I will be a little disappointed, but you would never know, I'm very polite.

[Carla]: I'm starting my own counter culture and the main fashion statement will be a monocle. Your openness to this trend leads me to believe we can definitely be friends.

You're polite? I thought you said you were kind of a jerk... I like**** jerks for some reason. I grew up with 4 alpha males, maybe it's just because that's what I'm accustomed to...

[Cajun]: Oh im a pretty huge jerk when I need to be, well... actually a lot of the time, but that doesn't mean I don't have manners. Four alpha males huh? Brothers? I have 2 brothers and the most alpha father of all time (the kind that can scare grown men with a look), so I learned from the best. You wouldn't be a match for me, although I'm always up for a challenge. Add me to Facebook, playing email tag on here is kind of lame. Cajun Spice, im the one relaxing with no shirt on the boat.

[Carla]: Yeah I have 3 older brothers and also one of the most alpha dads of all time.

Facebook shmacebook. I think that's cheating. Do you have MSN? Will you make fun of me if I tell you my email I've had since I was 14? These are all things I need to know.

[Cajun]: Cheating huh? I can't believe I've been denied a Facebook add, see now I think you're hiding something. Sure I have msn if you'd like to chat with me more, but Facebook was more so I could see what you really look like and if you have friends and are not a recluse etc. hahaha. You're missing out on all my wonderful moustache pics now too, I hope you're happy. Yes I will make fun of your msn email. What is it?

[Carla]: Hahaha! I'm not hiding anything, I just don't add whoever to Facebook. I only have genuine friends that I've met at least a few times on there. Plus... it could be weird if you added someone you don't know and then they posted something completely inappropriate for your mom to see. That's all.

I can send you more pics on msn if that's what you're after.

(she gives me her email)

bahahaha!

[Cajun]: Haha alright thats fair. Ill add you when I get back home later tonight, im going to a show now with a friend so we'll chat later! **** I don't even know your name.

[Carla]: Ok, sounds good. In the words of Hal Johnson and Joanne Mcleoad, keep fit and have fun.

I'm Carla. You are..

I get her on MSN and we have quite a long chat. I eventually get her number and we talk on the phone. This may not seem like much, but often when meeting normal women on dating sites you'll need to build a lot more comfort than usual in order to get them out, as was the case here with Carla. After that phone call she agreed to meet me the next night and we went for drinks. The whole process from messaging to meeting her took two or three days. Sometimes it may take weeks though, so if you think she's worth it, be patient.

Message Log 2 Jessica

#2 – Jessica "favourites" me, so I message her.

[Cajun]: So you're just going to favourite me and not even say anything? You want me to do all the work don't you? Well I'm not playing along until I know what you look like. You could be a 45 year old pedophile for all I know. Most filmmakers are... except me.

 She had no pictures listed on her profile. This can be a gamble sometimes, so I like to get pictures of them right away to see if I'm wasting my time. If there's enough attraction it's usually not too difficult to get them to send you a few.

[Jessica]: Dude. I was simply sorting through the truckload of babes on pof. You would have gotten a double take, eventually. so you're "extremely artsy. [You] act, write, draw, paint, sing, play instruments, make films and take photographs," but do you have anything to say for yourself? What kind of histories are you reading? I'm pretty into Rob Roy and the like right now.(For a grossly inaccurate/hhhhamazing interpretation of the story see "Rob

Roy," film (1995). And more seriously, post WWII Germany. There is a great film I just saw called "Germany, Pale Mother."

Also:

"i'm the guy who is perfectly comfortable making the first move; whether it be a

romantic kiss on the doorstep or throwing you up against a wall and making out

with you HARD... in the rain." (Yikes! intense/good visual.)

"I'm pretty mature for my age and am often labeled as 'Wise beyond my years' " (haha.)

"I have a fully black cat named Rod Stewart, he has bright green eyes and loves

women... just like me." (creepy/amazing.)

anyway hordaleski, here's some pics:

* She sends some pics and she's actually surprisingly cute.*

[Cajun]: Yeah, I don't really have anything to say for myself. Well, I do but I don't feel like typing it, I'm too lazy. Give me your number and I'll call and tell you, this message tag on a dating site is making me feel creepy...

She responds simply with her digits and I call her. Again, nothing special here but it's worth noting how I frame us messaging each other back and forth on a dating site as creepy. This will usually coerce women into escalating to a phone call under the threat of losing you and appearing creepy.

Message Log 3 Alexis

#3 – Alexis is fucking hot and has tattoos so I message her.

[Cajun]: So this weekend I was planning on robbing a bank, fleeing to the beach, driving into the water in a really dramatic way and faking my own death (SCUBA tanks in trunk). Wanna come? It's either going to be this weekend or next, so we can plan accordingly. You should probably make sandwiches too, BUT NOT EGG SALAD!! P.S. If you make egg salad and put CELERI in it, I will hate you forever.

~Derek

[Alexis]: Egg salad smells like farts. How do you feel about good ol' fashion P.B. & J? They make me nostalgic.

I should let you know, I have a weird phobia about getting water in my ears and nose so as long as you don't judge the ear plugs, nose plug, goggles and lime green bathing cap I'm in. Just looked at the schedule and next weekend is best for me because this week I'm practicing with my Norweigan death metal air band (We're getting really good!).

P.S. I never put celery in my egg salad. I prefer pickles.

-Alexis

*** She actually responded about three of four days later on new year's eve. This happens as many women will not check their mail every day. Don't feel like you need to match their wait times, I've often forgot to respond by doing that.***

[Cajun]: Shit! You caught me before I'm leaving to go to an east coast NYE party. Pickles!? that actually sounds good, and Norwegian DEATH metal??? is there any other kind? goggles are fine. we'll suit up like ducks. bring some records though, let's toss some Neil Diamond records as an act of defiance. I hate that guy! Happy new year! ill talk to you next year.

[Alexis]: What is your last name? Hopefully we are not related. All of my family is from the east coast. I will start hunting for a duck suit.

You have a happy New Years!

[Cajun]: I'm Acadian, ****** is my last name. I go to NB every summer, a bunch of us go down to get tubes and coast down the river all day, it's awesome! How was your new years eve?

[Alexis]: Ah my New years was great. started off as a two-man dance party and ended at the Odyssey on Davie. was fun. Yourself? How was your party? Did you go home for the Holidays? How long have you lived in

Van for? Hope you're doing better than I am today... .

[Cajun]: My NYE was a blast, ended up on a stage singing the band and drinking with a bunch

of friends. I just moved to Van 2 months ago, and most of my friends are from back

home in NB so they went home for the holidays. I stayed here because my cousin didn't

have enough money to return and I didn't want him to spend Christmas alone.

You seem cool, and I don't go on here that much, add me to Facebook if you have it:

Derek ******, I'm the one on the boat.

She added me to Facebook and I messaged her from there asking for her number, which I later turned into a date.

Message Log 4 Ardina

#4 – Ardina is a hot Brazilian so I message her.

[Cajun]: Next weekend I was thinking of robbing a bank, fleeing down to the ocean, driving off a cliff into the water and faking my own death (SCUBA tanks in trunk) Wanna come? You may need to drive though, as I was hoping to be able to throw Neil Diamond records at the cops from the passenger side window. It Would be an act of defiance, also I hate Neil Diamond. You should also bring sandwiches in case we need a snack break, no egg salad though, it smells like farts.

~Derek

[Ardina]: well actually I was thinking of robbing lululemon, they have way more money than a bank

and I'd definitely frisbee a few records, but I got that darn carpel tunnel from too much ultimate frisbee marathons this summer, still recovering. ice helps though.

and really? sandwiches?? come on, get with the times, its wraps and panenis now (not even sure how to spell that last one) hehe

~Ardina

[Cajun]: I don't get with the times, the times get with me. I am a devout sandwich enthusiast. You play Ultimate Frisbee? Ultimate frisbee makes me think of things like Dave Mathews, Jack johnson and Ben Harper. Also white people. I prefer frisbee golf, it's a more relaxed pleasure. Or jetski frisbee, thats a good one too. Hey what's your background? You have an interesting look.

[Ardina]: I was completely kidding about the ultimate frisbee

I just find it funny that people play such a well named 'sport'

usually in kits or spanish banks (whatwhitepeoplelike)

never tried frisbee golf. although recently just played soccer golf in thailand-amazing idea

'interesting look'

should I say thank you? or be concerned?

east indian/brazillian

but no one can ever guess the second part, so I usually leave it out.

I get more mistaken for italian,greek, and lately egyptian-whatever that means.

and yourself? heh

[Cajun]: I'm Acadian, which pretty much means a mix of French and Native. I only have a little native though, so I'm mostly french. by interesting look I really meant "Sexy look" but I didn't really want to be that forward so soon. But yeah, it's good. I haven't really met too many people off this site, and I just moved to Vancouver. It seems more normal here though than other places. I think it might be really hard to meet people in this city in normal ways. Although im not entirely sure yet. I've mostly been stuck in my room trying to finish writing this damn book! Damnit! I should be writing right now. How has your experience with guys on this site been so far?

At this point I know she's interested in me and I don't have to game really anymore so since I'm bored I decide to get some info out of her about her dating experiences for my own curiosity.

[Ardina]: just moved here eh

mmm fresh meat

kidding

where from originally?

I've met 3 guys off here- one wouldn't look away when I talked, barely blinked and he had no wit or sarcasm in him

the other was way too touchy right off the bat

the other was cool turned into concert buddies which I don't mind.

I do think it's hard to meet people here if you're new to Van cause everyone is in their little clique and too serious about life to be friendly and allow the new in. change seems hard for Van people.

I want to ask what your book is about, but I'd prefer hearing that answer in person-if you'll share.

[Cajun]: Yeah for sure! It's actually pretty funny what it's about. Let's stop playing email tag on this site though, it's kind of lame to me still. Give me your number and Ill call you tomorrow. Also, add me to Facebook if you like so you know im not a crazy person, my name is Derek _____, im the one on the boat haha.

[Ardina]: sounds good

I'm around all day

604-***-****

Chapter 10: Chat Logs

Escalating the interaction to a more personal medium is something you're going to want to do as soon as possible. The longer you stay on the dating site throwing messages back and forth the staler the interaction is going to become. You need to constantly be pushing the interaction forward at the most optimal speed. That means that if you think you can get her number, then you should, however in some cases the attraction required to get a number just isn't there and you need to do the next best thing. Instant messaging acts as a good bridge between dating site emails and the phone, and is usually an easy way to escalate the interaction with a very slim chance of rejection. I've provided several pages of my chat logs so you can get an idea of how to create attraction and escalate.

Chat Log 1 Katy

Katy has some really hot pics on her profile, I'm drunk so I sort of go direct (I was lazy really) and tell her to add me to msn so we can talk in real time. She does...

[Katy]: oh! Hi Derek!

[Katy]: how are you!?

[Derek]: IM GOOD

[Derek]: I saw you   -->(she sent me a picture with her dog)

[Derek]: You looked pretty good

[Katy]: yeah I'm alright

[Katy]: lol

[Derek]: whats your dog's name?

[Katy]: Papi

[Derek]: AHAHAH

[Derek]: Thats my name when im a grandfather

[Derek]: I want to be a pappy

[Katy]: no, papi

[Katy]: like spanish

[Derek]: Oh...

[Katy]: aiiiiiiiii papi!!!!!!!!

[Derek]: thats pretentious

[Katy]: indeed

[Derek]: haha how old?

[Katy]: He's 3

[Katy]: he bites everyone in the face

[Derek]: I love your dog

[Katy]: me too!

[Katy]: he bit my mom in the face when she was here visiting

[Katy]: she called me and told me it was her fault

[Katy]: I love my dog

[Derek]: like broke skin?

[Derek]: Yeah Rod does that too

[Katy]: they can't help themselves for some reason

[Derek]: Except Rod never bites faces, only everywhere else

[Derek]: He bit my buddie's dick once

[Derek]: everyone laughed

[Katy]: hahahahaha

[Katy]: even the dude with the cat bitten dick?

[Derek]: No, he died.

[Katy]: that's a heartwarming story

[Katy]: even more so

[Katy]: now that you mentioned he passed away

[Derek]: He got gangerine on his dick

[Derek]: is gangerine even real?

[Katy]: no

[Katy]: I think someone made it up

[Derek]: yeah me too, my mom probably

[Katy]: my mom told me that if you peed in the pool the water would turn pink and everyone would know

[Derek]: it doesnt?

[Katy]: so the next time we went to the pool of course I peed

[Katy]: and found out she was a LIAR

[Katy]: just to prove to her that I knew she was lying

[Derek]: I like your style

[Katy]: I like your beard

[Derek]: oh yeah you saw it!

[Katy]: I did!

[Derek]: it commanded your attention didnt it?

[Katy]: you have no idea

[Derek]: its very righteous

[Katy]: mostly because I didn't tell you yes or no

[Derek]: yes or no what?

[Katy]: nothing

[Derek]: your eyes said no

[Derek]: but your heart said yes

[Katy]: au contraire

[Katy]: my eyes always say yes

[Katy]: and my heart is usaully frozen solid

[Derek]: You is cold as ice

[Katy]: ice cold

[Derek]: it's your dark gift

[Katy]: it's my presence more than my gift

[Katy]: Ummmm

[Katy]: I have to tell you something

[Derek]: did i get you pregnant?

[Katy]: you may never want to speak to me again

[Katy]: yes

[Derek]: fuck...

[Katy]: but that's not what I needed to tell you

[Derek]: Oh ok, what is it then?

[Katy]: I'm a filthy smoker

[Katy]: I don't drink

[Katy]: or do drugs

[Derek]: *click*

[Katy]: but i smoke cigarettes

[Katy]: and it's gross

[Katy]: and I'm sorry

[Derek]: I just vomited all over my screen

[Katy]: I figured as much

[Derek]: I don't really care too much

[Katy]: you should

[Katy]: don't you want a healthy baby?

[Derek]: You're right

[Katy]: you knocked me up on skype chat

[Katy]: wow

[Derek]: I should have worn protection

[Katy]: now I know what the doctor meant when he told me I could get pregnant just by looking at boys

[Katy]: by boys he meant Derek

[Derek]: how long have you smoked for?

[Katy]: a long time

[Derek]: 20 years?

[Katy]: do we have to talk about it?

[Derek]: are you self conscious about it?

[Katy]: yes

[Derek]: good

[Katy]: I'm not self consious about many other things

[Derek]: are you self conscious about... .your bum?

[Katy]: funny you should mention that

[Katy]: it's the thing I'm LEAST self conscious about

[Derek]: Nice!

[Derek]: This is good news

[Katy]: yeah, I don't have many body part hang ups

[Katy]: I could walk around naked no problem anywhere

[Katy]: I do

[Derek]: me neither, except my GIGANTIC HEAD

[Katy]: wait...

[Katy]: oh... like your actual head

[Derek]: no, I mean my penis

[Derek]: I have a black man's penis

[Katy]: yes, so it's big?

[Derek]: Well, it's black. My penis is the colour black.

[Katy]: hahaha

[Katy]: that's awesome, you're hilarious.

[Katy]: nice moves

[Derek]: so you know, if it makes an appearance, things get messy

[Derek]: stains everywhere

[Katy]: I can imagine

[Katy]: but I'd prefer not to

[Katy]: so.... it's getting late. I need to lay down.

[Katy]: You're fun though, I want to keep talking.

[Derek]: Give me your number I'll call you and tuck you in.

[Katy]: Good idea, ###-###-####, call in like 5 mins.

[Katy]: before I go

[Katy]: I just want to say

[Katy]: I bought a violin for 10 dollars today

[Derek]: oh wow!

[Derek]: we should jam

[Katy]: yes

[Katy]: in about 12 years when I learn how to play it

[Derek]: Oh I wasn't talking about that

[Katy]: haha tease! alright talk to you in 5

[Derek]: haha ok

I call her and we talk for 15-20 mins continually escalating until I mention I need to go out to get milk and may be in her area if she's still awake. She says she may still be up and I should call her when I get there. I end up going over and spending the night.

Chat Log 2 Maggie

Maggie is a woman who messaged me and I ended up adding her to skype with my first reply by saying "Haha you seem fun, I hate this site and refuse to play message tag on it, add me to skype!" This is the chat conversation we have.

[Derek]: (awkward silence)

[Maggie]: I'm so relaxed!

[Maggie]: awkwardness relaxes me

[Derek]: me too, my rocks right noe

[Derek]: no typos there

[Maggie]: no

[Maggie]: I got it

[Maggie]: mer spoon alms

[Derek]: crotte de boueff

[Maggie]: splendid!

[Derek]: do you speak french?

[Maggie]: oui

[Maggie]: that means yes right?

[Maggie]: lol

[Derek]: No

[Derek]: Ben oui

[Maggie]: Ah

[Maggie]: Ben

[Maggie]: charming

[Derek]: Jai besoin un beer c'est right now la

[Maggie]: I actually don't speak french

[Derek]: You have shamed me

[Maggie]: No,

[Maggie]: you have shamed yourself

[Derek]: oh ok

[Maggie]: if it weren't for that damned beard!!!

[Derek]: Good

[Derek]: I'm going to rub it all over you

[Maggie]: mmmm

[Derek]: all over your eyes

[Maggie]: mmmmmmmmmmm

[Derek]: so you can see it

[Maggie]: mm?

[Derek]: yes

[Maggie]: exactly

[Derek]: Does your dad have a beard?

[Maggie]: no

[Derek]: moustache?

[Maggie]: no

[Derek]: your dad sucks so far

[Maggie]: he had a beard in his memoir of the early years

[Derek]: memoirs

[Derek]: hmmm

[Maggie]: I concur

[Derek]: what are you doing tomorrow

[Maggie]: well, I was thinking of waking up, eating something, putting on clothes and then walking out the door

[Maggie]: not sure what after that though

[Maggie]: that's as far as I got

[Derek]: Lets have a beach party

[Maggie]: where can we buy sand

[Maggie]: and a sandbox

[Maggie]: I would like to turn my apartment into the beach

[Derek]: Oh yeah we can be like Brian Wilson and write music in a sandbox

[Derek]: Early beach boys is pretty much my favourite band

[Maggie]: I like Sting

[Maggie]: hahaha

[Derek]: OH FUCK! STING!!!!

[Derek]: Sting is a legend

[Maggie]: like McGuyver

[Derek]: Yeah, Sting rocks

[Maggie]: totally

[Derek]: he lives in a castle and has tantric sex all day

[Maggie]: yeah...

[Maggie]: I know

[Derek]: I don't think you really do

[Maggie]: it's something we should all aspire to

[Derek]: I'm having tantric sex right now.

[Maggie]: Pfff you don't even know the MEANING of tantric sex.

[Derek]: Of course I do, what a silly thing to say.

[Maggie]: Have you ever tried it?

[Derek]: Thats when I put my bird in a girl's asshole right?

[Maggie]: Bingo.

[Derek]: Haha, but actually yeah I have tried tantric, only works with certain women though, and I've yet to do it in a castle.

[Maggie]: I agree, also you shouldn't bash anal.

[Derek]: Did I bash it?

[Maggie]: No, but I detected sarcasm.

[Derek]: Anal is great, but only when it's mutual.

[Maggie]: When is it not? I don't think a lot of women realize what they're missing.

[Derek]: Yes yes, it's always the same story until the beast is unleashed and then... second thoughts.

[Maggie]: Second thoughts?

[Derek]: Bit off more than you could chew.

[Maggie]: Pfff I doubt it. That would make it better if anything, I've yet to meet my match.

[Derek]: Well then, I'd like to meet you and your cavernous asshole.

[Maggie]: Bahahah I can't believe you said that! Do you have a 12 inch dick or something?

[Derek]: This conversation is getting pretty R rated for skype. Let's continue on the phone. What's your number?

[Maggie]: hmmmm, ok give me your number. I'll call you.

[Derek]: ###-###-#### give me a minute though, I'm going to get a drink.

[Maggie]: Me too, talk to you in 5!

She calls, we talk about sex and other dirty shit we'd like to do to each other. She comes over after 30 mins and spends the night.

Chat Log 3 Erika

I met Erika out one night, we talked in the bar for about 15 minutes then she had to leave with her friends. I told her what I did for a living (dating coach) and she though it was interesting, I got her number and Facebook add. Outside of a text or two, this was our first conversation since meeting that night. (Facebook chat very late the next night)

[Erika]: So why are you single?

[Derek]: I travel a lot for work, I just moved here, recently got out of a long-term relationship, and I'm super picky.

[Derek]: why are you single?

[Erika]: haha

[Erika]: I got out of a long relationship about 9 months ago

[Erika]: and I haven't been dating

[Derek]: I see

[Erika]: I'm also EXTREMELY picky

[Erika]: like, retardedly

[Derek]: yeah you seem like it

[Derek]: I like that

[Erika]: if you can be, you should

[Erika]: ;)

[Erika]: worst winky face ever

[Derek]: yeah one of the worst

[Derek]: we should see each other tomorrow. **normally would chat a bit longer before suggesting, or even wait until I called her to ask, but I was bored, and wanted to cut to the chase.**

[Erika]: I think we should

[Erika]: I was going to tell you abou this book though

[Derek]: Which book?

[Erika]:The Art of Seduction.

[Erika]: forgot to tell you about it the other night

[Derek]: art of seduction yeah I've read that.

[Erika]: I read it again recently and realized that I unconsciously did all of those things

[Derek]: ooooooh

[Erika]: it was kooky

[Derek]: you've been doing it to me all night.

[Derek]: with your sexy eyes

[Derek]: and your sexy face

[Erika]: lol

[Erika]: you should come see me in person

[Derek]: *says something grizzled*

[Derek]: I will

[Erika]: a wise man once said "if you want my body and you think I'm sexy, come on baby let me know"

[Erika]: I think it was Shakespeare

[Derek]: I hope you realize how significant that quote is considering my cat's name is Rod Stewart, and he just purred.

[Erika]: haha

[Erika]: me too

[Derek]: ooooooooh

[Erika]: he and I are alike

[Erika]: we are both pussies

[Erika]: he's a bit furrier though I think

[Derek]: Erika, I want your body and I think your sexy, I thought you should know **Rod Stewart song lyric**

[Erika]: shhhh

[Erika]: it's ok

[Erika]: I know

[Derek]: It's late, but I feel like going for a drive, how's Burnaby looking this time of night?

[Erika]: Pretty fucking awesome.

[Derek]: I'll call you in like 5 mins.

[Erika]: Deals.

Pretty obvious what happened there, she sent quite a few obvious signals. Fun night.

Chat Log 4 Alyssa

Alyssa is a long fuse that I met online and ended up getting into an argument with on skype chat when we first met about my job. She's really hot so I decide to ping her.

[Derek]: who is the hottest rocker of all time

[Derek]: for you

[Alyssa]: well

[Alyssa]: that's tough

[Alyssa]: one sec

[Derek]: any time period

[Derek]: so, in their prime

[Alyssa]: oh dear

[Alyssa]: this is way harder than you'd think

[Derek]: springsteen?

[Alyssa]: no

[Alyssa]: definitely not

[Derek]: Jagger?

[Alyssa]: nope

[Derek]: Plant?

[Alyssa]: I'm watching morrison right now

[Alyssa]: trying to see...

[Derek]: oh fuck, I studied his body language

[Derek]: years ago

[Alyssa]: hmmm

[Derek]: he studied Marilyn monroe, greek heroes and gods and other sexual icons for his "look."

[Alyssa]: well maybe not my favorite... but definitely up there

[Derek]: ok who would it be then?

[Alyssa]: eff

[Alyssa]: I don't know!

[Alyssa]: too much pressure!

[Derek]: well, give me some of the ones that are up there, this is for something I'm writing, it's important.

[Alyssa]: I can think of like, actors

[Alyssa]: but for some reason it's hard to think of rockers

[Derek]: well any musician

[Alyssa]: teenage michael jackson

[Derek]: nice!

[Alyssa]: which is strange

[Alyssa]: but yeah

[Alyssa]: when he was still black

[Alyssa]: hot

[Derek]: He looked way cooler when he was black.

[Alyssa]: it's not his looks

[Alyssa]: it's his persona

[Alyssa]: he has this quiet charisma

[Derek]: ahhh I think I know what you mean.

[Alyssa]: I have a thing with eyes

[Derek]: What kind of thing?

[Alyssa]: I don't know...

[Alyssa]: I can't explain it

[Alyssa]: but it's like a sparkle

[Alyssa]: you know?

[Derek]: yeah

[Alyssa]: I always look for it in people's eyes

[Derek]: creative souls

[Alyssa]: yeah!

[Alyssa]: this fire

[Alyssa]: intensity

[Alyssa]: passion

[Alyssa]: sometimes I look too hard though

[Alyssa]: I make a lot of eye contact with people

[Derek]: don't hurt yourself

[Alyssa]: guys usually think I'm a lot more interested in them than I really am

[Derek]: uh oh

[Alyssa]: because of my eye contact

[Alyssa]: I'm looking for the sparkle!!!!

[Alyssa]: it's not my fault!

[Derek]: sparkles are rare

[Alyssa]: agreed

[Derek]: gotta look deeeeeeeep

[Alyssa]: um

[Alyssa]: so like

[Derek]: give me your number, im calling you tomorrow

[Alyssa]: ohhhh

[Alyssa]: cocky confident

[Derek]: yup

[Alyssa]: ###-###-####

[Derek]: ill need a nick name for you

[Alyssa]: I haven't had one since grade 7

[Alyssa]: and that one was lame

[Alyssa]: so I look forward to it

[Derek]: ill call you boo

[Derek]: what up boo

[Derek]: I like your face boo

[Alyssa]: um... .

[Alyssa]: you're kidding

[Derek]: I never kid.

[Alyssa]: OR

[Alyssa]: you're LL

[Derek]: got me

[Derek]: Its me LL

[Alyssa]: are you licking your lips

[Alyssa]: you always do!

[Derek]: ... ..yes

[Alyssa]: hottttt

[Derek]: Sup Alyssa, I got a question...

incoming roleplay escalation. Here I escalate under the pretense that I'm simply acting, or playing a character that is not myself. I get all the benefits of escalation without the possibility of her getting offended, since I was only playing.

[Alyssa]: yes LL?

[Derek]: When you gonna let me tap that?

[Alyssa]: Oh my!

[Derek]: I wanna tap dat sweet ass.

[Alyssa]: I bet, it is sweet isn't it?

[Derek]: Exquisite.

[Alyssa]: You gotta sing me a song first.

[Derek]: Bitch I aint got all night!

[Derek]: LL doesn't have time for that monkey-ass nigga singin shit. I wanna get up in dat ass NOW.

[Alyssa]: Well, you're halfway there...

[Derek]: I'm calling you now, chat is no fun unless you can hear how awesome I'm sounding being LL.

[Alyssa]: Alright, we can chat about my ass.

[Derek]: No doubt.

I call her, tell her I bet she's into ass worship. She denies it but obviously is, I go over and worship it. Boink!

Chat Log 5 Diane

Diane sends me a message on POF saying she thinks I'm a hot pirate asshole. We send a few messages back and forth and then I ask for her skype. We have this conversation on chat.

[Derek]: lets add each other to Facebook now

[Derek]: were cool and normal

[Diane]: Ok ok ok

[Diane]: BUT

[Diane]: no

[Diane]: I refuse

[Derek]: I dont post on walls dont worry

[Diane]: hahaha

[Diane]: it just takes some of the magic out of it

[Derek]: You're probably right

[Diane]: preconceived notions

[Derek]: ok fine

[Diane]: Derek has 10987 friends on Facebook

[Diane]: 85.9% are hot women

[Diane]: hmmm

[Diane]: lol

[Derek]: I only have 43 friends

[Diane]: I don't believe you!!

[Derek]: hahaha good

[Derek]: Because if that were true id be more worried

[Diane]: I envy those people

[Diane]: who clearly restrained themselves when choosing friends on fb

[Derek]: yeah me too

[Diane]: I kind of want to delete a lot of people I have on there

[Diane]: even people I do talk to

[Derek]: me too, I did actually

[Diane]: I'm just scared they'll find out and hate me

[Derek]: yeah, you could always say you deleted it and made a new profile and forgot to add them back

[Diane]: but... Derek... .

[Diane]: that would be dishonest

[Derek]: Yeah! Fun!!

[Diane]: you are a sourcerer

[Diane]: wow

[Diane]: I can't spell

[Derek]: interesting spelling

[Diane]: there's no spell check?

[Diane]: come ON!

[Derek]: someone who sources a lot

[Diane]: yes

[Derek]: a sourceror, I get it.

[Diane]: it was a pun of sorts

[Diane]: I knew you'd enjoy it

[Derek]: We're havin a lot of fun here, lets get married and have 12 children

[Derek]: 7 of which would be feral

[Derek]: because they got lost in the woods

[Diane]: inevitably, yes

[Derek]: feral kids can run faster anyways

[Diane]: and

[Diane]: they are hungry like the wolf

[Derek]: !! I just got double Duran'd!

[Diane]: literally

[Derek]: now duran duran is stuck in my head

[Diane]: that's what he said

[Diane]: there was supposed to be a question mark after that

[Diane]: but even then it didn't make sense

[Derek]: You shouldnt get alone with me, fyi

[Diane]: what does that mean?

[Derek]: It means i'm a scoundrel

[Diane]: I know

[Diane]: I can handle myself

[Derek]: we'll see

[Diane]: how exciting!

[Diane]: a challenge!

[Derek]: maybe I'm the one who should be scared?

[**Derek**]: you're not allowed to rape me

[Diane]: scared isn't the right word

[**Derek**]: im sensitive

[Diane]: new soap?

[**Derek**]: yeah...

[Diane]: happens

[Diane]: nothing to be worried about

[**Derek**]: good!

[Diane]: yes

[**Derek**]: ok im goin to bed

[Diane]: yes

[**Derek**]: ill call you tomorrow evening

[Diane]: I look forward to it

[**Derek**]: I need your number though retard.

[Diane]: Right! ###-###-####

[Diane]: sleep naked

[**Derek**]: I am

[Diane]: ok

[Diane]: good

[**Derek**]: hah! sweet dreams of me

[Diane]: or ice cream sandwiches

[Diane]: both equally tempting

[Diane]: bye

[**Derek**]: yum, bye!

Of course, not all chats end up in sex as you can see. This one did turn into sex the next night though.

Chat Log 6 Amelie

Amelie was a very interesting artsy girl I messaged off POF. It took a few messages but I got her skype add after some flirting.

[Amelie]: look! you're on my Skype!

[Amelie]: <3

[Derek]: Oh boy!

[Derek]: I was just looking at your pics actually

[Derek]: Well, your art

[Amelie]: oh!

[Amelie]: and?

[Derek]: Fuckin sucks shit ass

[Amelie]: Really? Thanks!

[Derek]: haha just kidding, I love it.

[Amelie]: I love making it

[Derek]: It reminds me of something that wes anderson would do for a special edition dvd or something

[Amelie]: I like the sounds of that.

[Derek]: Yeah it's good. You're in LA?

[Amelie]: I am.

[Derek]: My friend is still sleeping

[Derek]: Haha my friends are sleeping here too

[Amelie]: so I'm just laying in bed, bein' lazy

[Derek]: Im sitting on a giant buddha bag

[Amelie]: Sounds comfy

[Derek]: It is, what are you doing in LA today?

[Amelie]: we are going to this bbq.

[Amelie]: then riding a motorcycle down sunset

[Amelie]: then getting our tattoos

[Derek]: Oh man, that sounds hot

[Amelie]: and go to this party later

[Derek]: Who rides?

[Amelie]: it WILL be hot!

[Amelie]: my bestie, Cheyenne

[Amelie]: she is pretty much the raddest girl of all time.

[Derek]: Is she so rad she's righteous?

[Amelie]: Totally righteous.

[Derek]: how many tattoos do you have?

[Amelie]: four

[Amelie]: this will be five

[Derek]: Have you always lived in Van? Because some of your photos looked suspiciously too cool for vancouver

[Amelie]: hahaha.

[Amelie]: yeah.

[Amelie]: but i travel as much as possible

[Amelie]: so some of them might be other cities?

[Derek]: interesting. me too, in fact I think I'm away more than I'm home. Away feels like home

[Amelie]: i like that.

[Derek]: the past 4 years have been like that because I have the weirdest job of all time

[Amelie]: whats your job

[Derek]: Its a little embarassing

[Derek]: are you ready?

[Amelie]: yes

[Derek]: I teach men how to talk to women.

[Amelie]: Whaaaaat

[Derek]: Yeah, I know.

[Amelie]: What makes you able to be a teacher?

[Amelie]: Are you Will Smith?

[Derek]: Its similar to hitch yeah

[Amelie]: I think that's pretty awesome, is that what you wanted to do?

[Derek]: haha, no, I wanted to act, or be a writer. I still do that, that's probably what I'll end up doing in the long run.

[Derek]: and live on a boat

[Amelie]: amazing

[Amelie]: who are some of your favourite writers

[Derek]: old school: Hemingway, Dostoevsky

[Derek]: Defoe

[Amelie]: OK, so classics

[Derek]: Robinson Crusoe is my favourite book of all time

[Amelie]: excellent.

[Derek]: and I secretly want to be marooned

[Derek]: But with a girl, and lots of supplies

[Derek]: and maybe a monkey

[Amelie]: haha

[Amelie]: my aunt

[Amelie]: she lived on this tiny island

[Amelie]: off the coast of BC

[Derek]: cool!

[Amelie]: and you can only get there by helicopter

[Amelie]: I could hook us up.

[Derek]: what!?

[Amelie]: but it won't be very warm.

[Derek]: don't tease me like that

[Amelie]: I'm not kidding.

[Derek]: You seem fun

[Amelie]: I mean, there's a lighthouse.

[Derek]: lets talk on skype with video

[Amelie]: I can't, I'm in the pitch black

[Amelie]: and I will wake her up

[Derek]: What does blackness have to do with anything

[Amelie]: haha

[Amelie]: I dont know

[Amelie]: I cant talk though! It'll be too loud!

[Derek]: Because I'm in the black too, and my blackness is probably more black than yours. How much more black could yours be? the answer is none. None more black.

[Amelie]: None more.

[Derek]: Ok, well we're talking soon

[Amelie]: We'll see.

[Amelie]: also, not to sound like a total loser

[Derek]: I've been spending the last 2 days watching the BBC life series

[Amelie]: but it's weird how much men in different cities like me.

[Derek]: It's ok, I like losers

[Derek]: uhhh... .

[Amelie]: haha

[Derek]: *awkward silence*

[Amelie]: Why is that awkward!?

[Derek]: Because its funnier

[Amelie]: You are.

[Amelie]: Funnier.

[Derek]: None more funnier than you

[Amelie]: I will make none more talk.

[Derek]: WHAT!?

[Amelie]: WHAT!

[Amelie]: Joksters.

[Derek]: This is outrageous

[Amelie]: You are!

[Amelie]: Fight?

[Derek]: Yes please

[Amelie]: So strange, you are.

[Derek]: You should meet me in person

[Derek]: I want to meet you

[Amelie]: Lets!

[Derek]: I like eccentric creative people

[Amelie]: I think I fall under that crowd

[Derek]: It's a good crowd

[Amelie]: I agree

[Amelie]: most of my friends fall under said crowd

[Derek]: me too, I need to surround myself with people like that

[Amelie]: Your whole part of "making the first move and pushing someone against a wall" part

[Amelie]: was a good part of your profile.

[Amelie]: Just sayin'

[Derek]: Yeah im pretty upfront with my intentions

[Amelie]: Well, you can be

[Amelie]: apparently

[Amelie]: you know when a girl wants it

[Amelie]: hahaha

[Derek]: I think its instinctual. Society just tells men that its wrong.

[Derek]: I don't see anything wrong with mutual desire

[Derek]: as long as its mutual

[Amelie]: Me neither.

[Amelie]: I am incredibly sexual.

[Amelie]: I have to quams about it

[Derek]: Well then you've met your match

[Amelie]: no

[Amelie]: Ha.

[Amelie]: I mean, I am INCREDIBLY sexual.

[Derek]: I don't feel the need to repeat myself

[Amelie]: hahaha

[Derek]: Im pretty confident you're no match for me

[Amelie]: hm.

[Amelie]: fine!

[Derek]: Don't tempt me!

[Derek]: I will melt you!

[Amelie]: Pft.

[Amelie]: I have done things you can't even IMAGINE.

[Derek]: Well, we need to play a game when I get back to Van

[Derek]: To see how the REAL master is

[Amelie]: What sort of game

[Derek]: It's a game taking turns asking questions

[Derek]: pretty simple

[Amelie]: Ok.

[Derek]: we'll make the rules up as we go

[Amelie]: I can do that.

[Derek]: Hmmm

[Derek]: you might win though

[Amelie]: Ohhh

[Amelie]: confidence draining?

[Derek]: No, but the way to win is to ask a question the other won't answer

[Amelie]: Interesting

[Derek]: You seem pretty competitive

[Amelie]: I will answer anything, I think.

[Derek]: See thats the problem

[Amelie]: I can't really think of anything you could ask

[Derek]: So, im going to need to think of some good ones

[Amelie]: that I wouldnt answer

[Amelie]: with great detail

[Derek]: Uh huh

[Derek]: I can think of a few

[Amelie]: Ask one now.

[Derek]: Ok, Ill start easy

[Amelie]: Ok.

[Derek]: When was the last time you masturbated?

[Amelie]: last night.

[Amelie]: before bed.

[Derek]: In bed?

[Amelie]: Yes.

[Derek]: Hmm ok

[Derek]: your turn

[Amelie]: What did you think about the last time you masturbated?

[Derek]: Haha you're going to think this is weird

[Amelie]: Nope.

[Derek]: I make up women in my head

[Amelie]: Nah, I do that, but with guys

[Derek]: Ahh ok, yeah although im not going to lie, after seeing some picture of you the idea crossed my mind

[Amelie]: I'm into it.

[Amelie]: Ok, your turn.

[Derek]: hmm

[Derek]: How many guys have you been with?

[Amelie]: 10

[Derek]: what about the ones that didnt count?

[Amelie]: haha

[Amelie]: didn't count, how?

[Derek]: "too drunk" "accident" etc

[Amelie]: 10

[Derek]: Haha, I know all the tricks

[Amelie]: How many men have you been with?

[Derek]: 0 im pretty hetero

[Derek]: maybe too hetero

[Amelie]: what about all the ones that didnt count?

[Amelie]: "too drunk" "accident" etc

[Derek]: Oh I see what you did there

[Amelie]: hhaha

[Derek]: Yeah, 0 unfortunately

[Derek]: well... fortunately

[Amelie]: interestin

[Amelie]: your go

[Amelie]: you said unfortunately.

[Amelie]: i screen shot that.

[Derek]: Ahahaha

[Derek]: craziest place you've ever had sex?

[Amelie]: hahaah :)

[Amelie]: Ummm... on top of a roof when it was snowing

[Amelie]: it was pretty crazy

[Derek]: Oooh cool!

[Amelie]: Yeah

[Amelie]: and hot, not literally, but.. yea

[Amelie]: you?

[Derek]: not allowed asking the same questions

[Derek]: Im making that rule up now

[Amelie]: oh, ok

[Amelie]: deal

[Derek]: try again

[Amelie]: How many girls have you been with

[Derek]: I already asked you that

[Amelie]: You asked guys

[Derek]: Hmm, usually i wouldn't let that pass, but you don't seem like someone who would care anyways.

[Amelie]: uhh nope

[Derek]: im not sure

[Amelie]: now you will never know how many women ive been with

[Derek]: but a lot

[Amelie]: a lot, hey?

[Derek]: hmmm over 200, I couldn't tell you exactly

[Amelie]: Impressive, ok your turn.

[Amelie]: ask me a good one

[Derek]: On a scale of 1 to 10

[Amelie]: ...

[Derek]: how would you rate yoru oral skills?

[Derek]: BAM!

[Amelie]: as an average?

[Derek]: yeah

[Amelie]: i'd say 8.8

[Amelie]: maybe 9.2

[Derek]: This is impressive

[Amelie]: sometimes I get lazy

[Amelie]: but I don't have a gag reflex, and I enjoy cum

[Amelie]: so it gets me a high average.

[Derek]: yes, that would

[Amelie]: are you into anal?

[Derek]: Kind of

[Amelie]: you are a dork

[Amelie]: Kind of?

[Derek]: Well kind of in that it depends on the ass

[Amelie]: hha

[Amelie]: Interesting

[Derek]: Or, the owner of said ass

[Derek]: Im more of a giver

[Derek]: I get off getting others off

[Amelie]: Same.

[Amelie]: ha

[Amelie]: ok! your turn!

[Derek]: Hmmm

[Derek]: Whats the one thing you've always wanted to try, sexually, but haven't?

[Amelie]: I think fake raped.

[Amelie]: Like having someone come into my house

[Amelie]: that I know

[Derek]: Look behind you... .

[Amelie]: and holding me down and all that nonsense..

[Derek]: Yeah, I can see the appeal

[Amelie]: yeah

[Derek]: have you read wuthering heights?

[Amelie]: What's one thing you've tried sexually and didn't like?

[Amelie]: (no..)

[Derek]: Ok, well you should, anyways, a fake rape happens in that, and its pretty much the quintessential romance novel

[Derek]: Hmmm

[Derek]: S&M

[Derek]: Well, she was more into cock n ball torture I think

[Derek]: that didn't last long

[Amelie]: eek

[Amelie]: yeah

[Derek]: This is an interesting conversation

[Amelie]: Haha

[Amelie]: Yeah

[Derek]: We're getting to know each other pretty intimately

[Amelie]: Yeah, we are, I think that's a good way to get to know someone, sometimes.

[Derek]: Sometimes...

[Derek]: This time yes

[Derek]: hey do you have Facebook?

[Amelie]: I do.

[Derek]: let's be friends on that

[Amelie]: Ok

[Amelie]: feel free to add me

[Derek]: Im Derek _____

[Amelie]: ok

[Amelie]: added

[Amelie]: have fun lurking me

[Amelie]: i am a ridiculous person.

[Derek]: I kind of already have with yoru pics, I figure you should do the same

[Amelie]: haha

[Amelie]: deal

[Derek]: Ok im lurking now

[Amelie]: samesies

[Derek]: nice butt

[Amelie]: nice beard

[Amelie]: wait, butt?!

[Derek]: thats right

[Amelie]: where can you see my butt

[Derek]: In your undies

[Amelie]: oh

[Derek]: It's a side butt

[Amelie]: prbs

[Amelie]: i am a total dork

[Amelie]: and i get pictures taken of me

[Amelie]: being a total dork

[Derek]: Yeah, I figured that out

[Derek]: It's good though

[Amelie]: I agreeee

[Derek]: I tend to make weird faces in pics on purpose

[Amelie]: you're a shorty, arent you

[Derek]: I think im 5'7 or 5'8, but yeah, im short

[Amelie]: shawty

[Derek]: how tall are you!?

[Amelie]: 6'2

[Amelie]: ahahaha.

[Amelie]: 5;8

[Derek]: How deep are you?

[Amelie]: what does that mean!?!

[Derek]: Hahahah

[Amelie]: like vaginal cavity?

[Amelie]: or emotionally?

[Derek]: sure

[Amelie]: I'd say I'm deep both ways.

[Derek]: This is great news

[Amelie]: why

[Derek]: Well, I need to know these things in case we get physical

[Derek]: Because I have a black dick

[Amelie]: haha

[Derek]: It's the colour black

[Amelie]: haha

[Amelie]: my ex was 6'2 black man,

[Amelie]: so..

[Amelie]: there's that.

[Derek]: Haha we're dirty

[Amelie]: Yup!

[Amelie]: I am a total perv.

[Derek]: Im just trying to see if I can say something that you would find forward

[Amelie]: Results?

[Derek]: Well, that would be up to you

[Amelie]: Nope.

[Derek]: I think no though

[Derek]: ask me something now

[Amelie]: hmm ok.

[Amelie]: Lets see.

[Amelie]: Are you into big tits?

[Derek]: no, WHY DO YOU HAVE THEM? **She has insanely huge tits for her size**

[Amelie]: nope

[Amelie]: I am pretty flat.

[Derek]: Good

[Amelie]: I am also a size 4

[Amelie]: YEAH WHATEVER

[Amelie]: IM A BIG LADY

[Derek]: Hahah

[Derek]: I like women with full figures

[Amelie]: With huge titties?

[Derek]: Im more an ass man, but yeah tits are nice

[Amelie]: yeah

[Amelie]: I have a nice ass, too

[Derek]: we'll see

[Amelie]: so there's that..

[Derek]: I've only seen a profile

[Amelie]: here: **link**

pic of butt

[Derek]: Thats a nice butt!

[Amelie]: thanks!

[Derek]: See, now when we meet each other were just going to be thinking sexual thoughts

[Amelie]: I wouldve been anyway.

[Amelie]: Most of my thoughts are sexual.

[Derek]: Yeah, me too

[Derek]: At least we're honest

[Amelie]: It's true

[Amelie]: I better get going though

[Amelie]: its 1pm

[Derek]: Yeah me too

[Amelie]: and i have tattoos to get, motorcycles to ride

[Derek]: I need to eat dinner!

[Amelie]: hhaha

[Derek]: Have fun Amelie!

[Derek]: Let's talk soon

[Amelie]: i need to eat lunch!

[Amelie]: I will

[Amelie]: deal!

[Derek]: We should set up a call date

[Amelie]: see you

[Amelie]: lets.

[Derek]: Ok ill message you with deets

[Amelie]: I wont be home until Monday night

[Amelie]: ok

[Amelie]: see you!

[Derek]: See ya!

Dating Site Pro Tips

I figured I would make a quick list for those of you who want a bit of an extra edge. Some of these have been mentioned in the book already, some haven't, and quite a few come from women themselves.

Here's a trick if you live in a small town and have a couple friends to help you out. Three friends of mine did this in their hometown because there were only about 30-40 women on the dating site, and they would hardly respond since there were so many more guys. So they did an experiment and set up over 50 fake profiles of women, being very meticulous about making sure they seemed like real profiles and using attractive pictures. The guys would manage the fake profiles by answering messages and messaging dudes for about two weeks, long enough to get all their attention. Then they would message only the hot (real) women with their real profiles and end up getting responses since nobody else was messaging them. It worked!

Keep changing your main profile picture until you receive the most consistent responses.

Set up accounts in cities you plan to visit. That way you can line up dates for when you're there.

Never invite a woman over to your house on a first date. Wait until you're sure she's normal. This may take more than one date.

I would advise against sleeping with someone who you think may be unstable, even if they're gorgeous. You may think it's good experience, but the repercussions could be damaging.

If your buddies have also read this book and are in the same city, make sure you're not using the same lines and messages on the same women.

If you want a good photo try taking some HD video and then going over it and choosing a good frame. This applies if you have a good camera with HD video.

If you and your buddies are all using this info in a smaller city, keep tabs on women so you can give them a rundown if they happen to date the same one.

Keep tabs on the women you've messaged so you don't send the same opening message over and over to the same woman and blow your cover.

If you're experimenting with openers, and one works, write it down so you can test it again. Have a sheet with all your successful ones so you can bring them out in an emergency.

Find a cool place in town that has cheap drinks and a nice atmosphere.

Every city has one. Make this your go to place if you'd like to date often but don't have much cash.

Make friends with the servers and bartenders in your favourite date locations. Get their names, tip them nicely, and open them warmly every time you see them (especially on the date)

Create a fake profile on a dating site pretending to be a woman. You'll need to find some public domain pics of an attractive woman to do this legally. Peruse male profiles and when you see one that you think is a natural or simply very well done, *like*, *favourite*, or *poke* him and see what he sends you as a message. This can give you some valuable insights from naturals.

Try out different dating sites to see which is the most popular. Different countries and cities have sites that are more popular than others.

Don't be afraid to befriend women who you may not connect with romantically after a date. You never know who she may be friends with.

Afterword

I mentioned in the introduction to this book that online dating should not in any way replace your daily regiment of actually going out and working on your social skills. As I said earlier, it should be used to augment your abilities, and I think that's worth repeating now. The guys who get great at the art of seduction are the guys who learn to never turn it off. They charm everyone they meet, in any situation, for nothing more than to prove to themselves that they can. They're constantly working on their ability to seduce, seeing it more as a lifestyle or personality type than a means to an end.

From my experience, it seems that most men who want more women in their life see online dating as the first step. It's definitely one of the easiest ways to meet more women, and now with the help of this book you should have no problem doing so, but this is still only the beginning. Having more women in your life will mean nothing if you do not possess the strength of character to keep them. This is something you can only achieve by *becoming* an attractive character, as opposed to *appearing* like one, which is what this book has taught you. Don't get me wrong, the experiences that this book will lead you to will give you the foundation of confidence and positive beliefs to make going forward much easier, but it will not do it for you. You must incorporate the lessons from this book into your everyday life, in every interaction you have, on a daily basis if you can.

When I first moved to Toronto, I made a point to get to know every person in my neighbourhood that I knew I would see on a regular occasion. The guy who works at the convenience shop across the street, the bank tellers at my bank, the cashiers in the grocery store; I wanted to get to know *everyone*. This never amounted to anything more than attempting to have a *real* conversation with them, sometimes topics as bland as the weather or local happenings injected with all the wit, charm and personality I could muster. I would learn their names after a few meetings, and then open them warmly every time I saw them. Like they were old friends. After a few weeks of doing this, they would have beaming smiles every time I walked in to see them; I became part of their *community*.

This has tremendous value outside of simply forcing yourself to be more social. When you enrich these people's lives with your friendship they tend to do the same for you. Mike, who owned the convenience store across the street, would give me deals on products that "fell off trucks" (this was in family run little Portugal) from time to time. Mibrek, an older Egyptian woman who owned the falafel shop that I ate at regularly, ended up setting me up with her daughter who had just moved from Egypt and wanted to see the city. We ended up dating for a little while before she ended up moving back home. Ray and Charlie, the gay couple that ran the antique store/auction house, would always call me whenever something came in that they knew I wanted, and offer it to me at a discounted price. The value of being sociable and friendly with people became so obvious that I now make a habit of doing this with every person that I meet, whether I think I'll see them again or not.

The other obvious benefit of engaging people on a regular basis is that it starts to alter your personality; you become a *sociable person.* Talking to the gorgeous brunette who walks by you on the street isn't so hard anymore when you've been talking to people all day. You start to enjoy conversing with random people because you build up the belief that everyone enjoys your company through actively experiencing this in your regular interactions. Start doing this everyday and your friends and family will start to notice you will appear happier and more confident. This is what women describe as *charm.*

Most men lead lives of quiet desperation, thinking: *"One day I'll be the guy I've always wanted to be, one day."* But this day never comes because they never decide to actually start being this person. They simply hope it will happen, in vain. You need to make a conscious choice to start becoming the man you've always wanted to be, the man inside. Who is this man? What would he say or do in any given situation? The only way to become him is to start living like him. He's inside all of us. I hope this book brings you the experiences you need in order to start becoming the man you've always always wanted to be, and I hope that the path it leads you to brings you the same happiness that it has brought me. Remember that online dating is only the beginning; what starts with taking a nice profile picture of yourself ends with total and utter contentment. I hope you all get there.

— *Derek "Cajun"*

www.ingramcontent.com/pod-product-compliance
Lightning Source LLC
Chambersburg PA
CBHW072226270326
41930CB00010B/2019